ELIZABETH ALLEN AND DANIEL VESTAL
EDITORS

# EXEMPLARS

## DEACONS AS SERVANT AND SPIRITUAL LEADERS

D1512323

Smyth & Helwys Publishing, Inc.
6316 Peake Road
Macon, Georgia 31210-3960
1-800-747-3016

*Library of Congress Cataloging-in-Publication Data*

Names: Vestal, Daniel, 1944- editor.
Title: Exemplars : deacons as servant and spiritual leaders / edited by
Daniel Vestal and Elizabeth Allen.
Description: Macon : Smyth & Helwys, 2016. | Includes bibliographical
references.
Identifiers: LCCN 2016022683 | ISBN 9781573128766 (pbk. : alk. paper)
Subjects: LCSH: Deacons.
Classification: LCC BV680 .E94 2016 | DDC 253--dc23
LC record available at https://lccn.loc.gov/2016022683

# Acknowledgments

Carol Younger is the primary author of sessions 1–3. Mike Smith is the primary author of sessions 4–6. Guy Sayles is the primary author of sessions 7–9. Elizabeth (Libby) Allen co-edited the material with me. A special group of deacons have been conversation partners and prayer partners from the beginning: Carol Palmer, Mike Hendley, Connie Jones, David Keel, Don Brewer, Susan Broome, and Mark Whittaker. Several ministers have offered their support and counsel: Philip Vestal, Frank Broome, Greg DeLoach, and Bob Patterson.

Hundreds of deacons contributed to this workbook in listening sessions, retreats, and conferences. They have responded to surveys and answered questions about their hopes, disappointments, and struggles in deacon ministry. Keith Gammons of Smyth & Helwys Publishing has been an encourager and adviser. From the beginning, this has been a collaborative project and a labor of love.

Carol Younger is a prolific writer and the editor of *Reflections*, a devotional magazine published by Smyth & Helwys. She has contributed to numerous books, periodicals, and Christian education curriculum. Her most recent book is *Mark: Finding Ourselves in the Story*, which she co-authored with her husband, Brett.

Mike Smith serves as senior pastor of Central Baptist Church in Fountain City, Knoxville, Tennessee. In addition to his pastoral work, he enjoys writing, editing, and golfing. His most recent book is *Beginnings: A Reverend and a Rabbi Talk About the Stories of Genesis.*

Guy Sayles is a tenured pastor, visiting assistant professor of religion at Mars Hill University, an adjunct member of the faculty at Gardner Webb University's Divinity School, and a consultant with the Center for Healthy Churches.

Elizabeth (Libby) Allen is the administrative coordinator for the Eula Mae and John Baugh Center for Baptist Leadership at Mercer University. She served for seventeen years with admissions for McAfee School of Theology, Mercer University, and was ordained as a deacon in 1986.

Daniel Vestal is the director of the Eula Mae and John Baugh Center for Baptist Leadership and is the Distinguished Professor of Baptist Leadership at Mercer University. He has served as a pastor and has been in leadership with a number of denominational, ecumenical, and institutional organizations.

# Contents

# Deacons as Servant and Spiritual Leaders

Daniel Vestal

It would not be an exaggeration to say that my life and ministry have been shaped by Christian laity as much as by Christian clergy. I love the church because it is the body of Christ. It is where class, rank, or title should not matter, where each of us is graced, called, and commissioned to be the continuing embodiment of Christ in the world. It is where we, both individually and corporately, are indwelt by the Spirit and are bound together into a mysterious unity in diversity that mirrors the Triune God.

In the churches where I have been a member and where I have served as a pastor, I have experienced the presence and power of God in dramatic and profound ways. I have watched the living and the dying of Christians whose names will never be widely known but whose witness changed the world. I have participated in a communion of saints who, although not perfect, were authentic exemplars of Christ. They represented and reflected the character of our Lord in beautiful ways, sometimes in dramatic fashion but most of the time in quite ordinary and everyday ways. Many of them were deacons.

It is because of their examples and friendships that I invite all deacons to imagine and reimagine what Christian discipleship might look like for them in today's world and in their particular contexts. In the past few years I have spent time with hundreds of deacons, listening to their convictions and concerns. I have listened to both their joy and their pain. One of the discoveries I have made is that deacons are serious about being deacons. They want to be effective and participate in the work of Christ's church in meaningful ways. But I have also discovered that, in many churches, the diaconate is ineffective and deacons do not feel that they are participating meaningfully in Christ's church.

On many occasions, I have heard deacons say, "Our deacon body is not sure about its identity and role," "We know who we don't want to be, but we're not sure we know who we do want to be," or "Everything seems to be changing in the church, and deacons are having a difficult time adapting to those changes," or "We want to be spiritual leaders in the church, but we aren't sure we know how."

## Deacons as Examples and Models

The only place in the New Testament where deacons are mentioned by name is 1 Timothy 3:8-13. The qualifications for their selection relate to Christian character and conduct as well as personal and public witness. Then there is this verse: "For those who serve well as deacons gain a good standing for themselves and also great confidence in the faith which is in Christ Jesus" (1 Tim 3:13, NRSV).

It seems clear that in the earliest Christian communities, deacons were *examples* and *models* of Christian discipleship. They were selected as deacons because they already bore the marks of Christ-likeness, and as they functioned in congregational leadership they demonstrated that same character.

In the early Jerusalem church, seven men were chosen to "serve tables," and though they are not named as deacons, it is clear that they are servant leaders within the church. The requirement for their selection is again that they are already *examples* and *models* of Christ-likeness, "of good repute, full of the Spirit and of wisdom" (Acts 6:3). To the Roman congregation the Apostle Paul writes a commendation of Phoebe, a "servant of the church," which could also be translated as a "deacon" of the church. She is commended because she is a "saint" and one who "has been a helper to many" (Rom 16:1-2). Again, it is her Christian disposition and behavior that makes her an *example* and *model* worthy of imitation.

I know that deacons today do not feel worthy of being compared to these New Testament deacons and would shudder at the thought of being called an *example* and *model* Christian. I imagine that the earliest deacons would have felt and said the same thing. They simply wanted to serve God in humble devotion and were willing to do whatever needed to be done in the church. And yet the fact remains that the New Testament describes these first deacons in terms of being *examples* and *models*. It is not just clergy who point people to Christ; it is laity as well, especially deacons. It is not just apostles, prophets, pastors, and evangelists who remind people of Christ; it is women and men who are willing to serve God by "waiting on tables."

## Deacons as Servants

Nowhere in the New Testament are specific deacon responsibilities offered. We simply know that the word "deacon" is the word for *servant*. Hence deacons are called, chosen, ordained to be servants—of God, of the church, and of people in need. Servanthood is to be their way of life because deacons' lives are modeled after the One who said of himself, "the Son of Man came not to be served but to serve" (Matt 20:28).

Deacons have a unique opportunity to be exemplars of Christ by imitating and incarnating his servant ministry. Just as Christ had compassion for people, so deacons have compassion for people. As Christ washed the feet of the disciples, so deacons wash the feet of others, either figuratively or literally. As Christ humbled himself without hubris and pretension for sacrificial ministry, so deacons humble themselves without hubris and pretension for sacrificial ministry. They emulate the lifestyle, attitude and love of Christ. They weep with those who weep and rejoice with those who rejoice.

Their tasks may be as menial as waiting on tables or as dramatic as becoming a martyr for Christ. In some ways their specific tasks are not ones they choose but ones that are chosen for them. The demands of the congregation, the needs of the world, and the conflicts and circumstances around them call on them to serve in diverse ways. And in this service, they extend the life and ministry of Christ. They extend Christ's kingdom. And they do it all to the greater glory of God.

## Workbook Scope and Sequence

This workbook was born from years of pastoral experience and, in more recent years, a growing conviction that congregational renewal must include lay renewal. Nearly every Baptist church I know has a diaconate, so it seems reasonable that if lay renewal is to happen, it must include deacon renewal. Perhaps deacon renewal could be an entry point for broader lay renewal. The colleagues who joined me in the writing of this workbook are tenured in congregational ministry, and we all share a deep love for deacons. We have observed a sincere desire among deacons to grow in their Christian discipleship and in their effectiveness as deacons.

The content and format of this workbook is designed to encourage robust conversation within diaconates as well as between deacons, clergy, and other laity. For deacons to reach their full potential as spiritual leaders, thoughtful and prayerful conversation must happen. All of us grow spiritually as we listen and speak to one another with open minds and loving hearts. This workbook was born and has been developed out of conversations, and it is offered with the prayer for the Holy Spirit to use it and the conversations it produces to renew today's church.

The purpose of this workbook is to encourage and inspire deacons to become spiritual leaders as they seek to be exemplars of Christ and servants of Christ's church. Those of us who form the writing team explored a matrix or framework for individual deacon development as well as formation for an entire diaconate. We believe the book can be helpful as a study guide for an individual deacon or, perhaps even better, used in a group format where deacons study together, hold one another accountable, and offer support for one another. The three dimensions of this matrix are as follows:

## Who Do Deacons Need to Be?

The first question has to do with the experiential and relational side of Christian discipleship. Life as a Christian is lived in relationship with the Triune God (Father, Son, Holy Spirit). It is personal because God is personal. And it is transformative because relationship with God will always be transformative. Relationships with people are also transformative. The experience of Christian discipleship in community with others who share this experience results in our becoming all that we were created and saved to be.

## What Do Deacons Need to Know?

The second question has to do with faith development and the more cognitive side of Christian discipleship. Faith has an object. Faith has content. So knowing requires learning and understanding. We are commanded to love God with our minds, and we are promised that "the truth will set us free" (John 8:32). Those who follow Jesus are called "disciples," which means we are "learners."

## What Do Deacons Need to Do?

The third question has to do with conduct and the behavioral side of Christian discipleship. Our actions in everyday life, and sometimes our non-actions, reveal our priorities, values, and commitments. What we actually do in the particular circumstances of our lives says a lot about our faith. Scripture refers to our actions as "deeds" or "works."

This three-part matrix is offered as an integrated approach to Christian discipleship requiring individual discipline, group trust, and shared dependence on God. The tendency in all of us is to focus on one of these dimensions. According to our temperament and circumstances, we are inclined to concentrate only on one instead of all three. Although these dimensions are presented in a linear and sequential fashion, they are inextricably tied to one another. They are like three strands to a rope or three legs to a stool. They simply cannot be considered alone or apart from the others.

# Who Do Deacons Need to Be?

The first question has to do with the experiential and relational side of Christian discipleship. Life as a Christian is lived in relationship with the Triune God. It is personal because God is personal. And it is transformative because relationship with God will always be transformative. Relationships with people are also transformative. The experience of Christian discipleship in community with others who share this experience results in our becoming all that we were created and saved to be.

## Session 1: Living Portraits Who Are Part of God's Masterpiece

This session, which inspires conversation about deacons being "works in progress," uses a parable to illustrate the different ways we see ourselves and one another. The metaphor of being "part of God's masterpiece" helps us see ourselves as individual masterpieces created by God and also as part of a greater masterpiece. The individual exercises and group questions are intended to help deacons see themselves from a divine perspective while also being honest about the gap between who we are created to be and how we live our lives.

## Session 2: Beloved Children of God Who Experience Grace

This session uses the parable of Luke 15 to inspire conversation about deacons as beloved children of God. The two sons in the parable, one prodigal and one self-righteous, are both loved and part of the same family. They also illustrate the need for continued conversion. The individual exercises and group questions are intended to help deacons have greater self-awareness and understand their life experiences in light of God's grace.

## Session 3: Members of Christ's Church Who Are Gifted with the Spirit

This session continues to use the parable of Luke 15 to inspire conversation about deacons as members of Christ's church who are gifted with the Spirit. No church is perfect, but to belong to Christ means to become a part of Christ's faith family. The individual exercises and group questions are intended to help deacons both celebrate their identity in the church and claim their giftedness for the church.

# Deacons Are Living Portraits Who Are Part of God's Masterpiece

## A Question We Need to Ask

Most of the time, exchanging information about who we are is easier than talking about who we need to be. We know how to polish our résumés and introduce ourselves to strangers. We share our best "selfies" with each other on Facebook, and post our results from the latest online personality test so the world will know what Star Wars character we are most like. We identify the families, schools, teams, and politics that shape us. We name our religious affiliations and list our work experiences. We are ready for any mandatory "get acquainted" game that requires naming the five adjectives that best describe ourselves, which personal trait is our favorite, or which three things we would save from a fire.

We get used to knowing a little information about a lot of people. Without realizing it, we learn someone's data but never know their story. Before long, we become too skilled at sharing facts about who we are while keeping hidden the truths that matter most to us.

Churches, on the other hand, are meant to celebrate and cultivate our stories. Becoming part of a congregation formed and shaped by Christ's story helps us proclaim, understand, and develop our own. When Christian communities are at their best, they move us beyond the facts of our lives and help us experience purpose and meaning. In a culture of virtual friendships, Christ's church must be more than a place where people know your name. Christ's church is the place that takes your story in, cherishes it, and helps you discover more of its meaning and possibility.

Does this describe your congregation? Are we being Christ's church in this story-embracing way? Churches, like the rest of us, face limitations. If we succeed in greeting visitors on a Sunday morning, if we remember their names and learn something about each one, we feel that we are a friendly church, which is no small thing. But do churches that are satisfied with knowing a little information about a lot of people fully experience the community that God intends for us to share? We can grow so comfortable with who we are that we never think about who we need to be.

Consider the following parable:

The Deacon Nominating Committee of First Church of the Parable gathers for its initial meeting. The committee chair calls on the persistent widow in Luke 18 to lead the opening prayer, which includes a long series of repetitive requests for God "to help us know who our deacons need to be." After a chorus of "Amens," the chair begins.

"As you can see from the long list of names on your handout, we received plenty of deacon recommendations. The good Samaritan was nominated most often, but a few folks are upset that he's not from here. Also, the merchant who sold everything for one precious pearl received several votes, but some are questioning whether he has anything left to tithe."

The committee looks at the other names on the list. One member clears her throat. "What do you think about this shepherd who left ninety-nine sheep alone to search for the one that was lost? I appreciate the sentiment, but couldn't that kind of leadership create chaos in our ministries?"

"Maybe that dedicated sense of mission should belong solely to Jesus, rather than a new deacon," someone suggests.

"What about these nominees who are listed as a group: early morning vineyard worker; 9:00 a.m. worker; noon worker; 3:00 p.m. worker; and 5:00 p.m. worker?" another member asks. "The nomination reads, 'I'm listing everyone in Matthew 20, because the landowner was on to something we need to learn.' But this troubles a lot of our people, who are saying that the latecomers haven't put in their time or proved their devotion. Not to mention that this gives one group of people too much power."

After a lengthy conversation about the five talents candidate and the two talents nominee, half of the committee convinces the others that the two should get equal consideration—despite the church's desperate need for extra talents. After all, both of them get equal praise in Matthew 25.

Each name on the list raises new questions. As the committee talks, the chair makes notes about which issues need further attention at the next meeting. Questions about background, personality, work style, decision-making skills, and length of church experience will make up the next agenda. Pleased with their progress, the chair mentions the last two names on the list, hoping for a brief discussion before they adjourn.

"Remember that we only select one deacon at a time from individual families. So which son in Luke 15, the older or the younger, is the deacon our church needs?" The chair's quick read of the room suggests that the majority of the group consists of firstborns, who will likely vote for one of their own.

A brief silence ensues like the calm before a storm. Advocates for the older brother unleash impassioned tributes to their candidate. They use words like "deacon material," "well respected," "hard working," and "responsible." When referring to the younger brother, they say words like "prodigal," "loose living," "feeding pigs," and "disgracing his dad." It bothers them that the younger son was even nominated. Someone in the corner starts mumbling "self-righteous," "unforgiving," and "joyless."

Eventually the speeches wind down. The chair tests the waters. "So, it sounds like we need the older brother's maturity? Any other comments?"

The mumbling member stands. His voice shakes, "The problem with Christianity today is that we have a prodigal son gospel in an older brother church." He can't remember who wrote this idea, or he would have used that name just to sound more authoritative. "We need deacons who treasure forgiveness, who have received it and give it freely. We need deacons who humbly seek God and who joyfully embrace God's love because they know they can't live without it. These spiritual experiences matter. As we choose our deacons, are we asking the right questions?"

Silence again. Then, this time, a different kind of energy starts filling the room. The committee sets the list of names aside and starts to discuss what hopes God may have for their church. They talk about who God wants them to become. The meeting unfolds in ways the chair did not expect. The conversation takes different forms, and no one seems ready to wrap things up. A few are looking over Luke 15 and debating whether or not the eldest went to his brother's party with his father. Three others brainstorm what questions to ask candidates about their spiritual lives. Two members share their faith-defining stories with each other.

The persistent widow smiles at her committee chair. Maybe this is God's response to their opening prayer. The meeting goes longer than expected, but no one seems to mind. They are discovering the heart of their work. God is helping them with the question, *"Who do our deacons need to be?"*

Like the nominating committee meeting of First Church of the Parable, our practical focus on questions like "Who needs to be a deacon?" often delays our conversation about "Who do deacons need to be?" The first question comes with a familiar action plan. It reminds us to kick off our annual efforts to identify and nominate those who have gifts to serve Christ through the church. It gives us deadlines so that we will finalize a slate of candidates before the church business meeting. The diligent members among us start rereading 1 Timothy 3 just to refresh their memories. If they study their commentaries on the passage, they remember that Paul's counsel here is not an exhaustive checklist for choosing deacons. Like Paul's lists of spiritual gifts in his other letters, these character-istics simply represent what faith-shaped lives look like, and why they help the church serve.

Church calendars are so full, and questions such as "Who needs to be a deacon?" take so much attention that we rarely find time to ponder seriously, "Who do our deacons need to be?" We start to think that both questions are asking the same thing.

That is, until one day when you are sitting in a deacons' meeting and find yourself wondering why you are there. You remember the conversation in which the nominating chair asked you to serve by saying that the committee thought 1 Timothy 3 sounded like you. Of course you said, "Yes." You glance at the friend sitting next to you and remember how you urged her to say yes, too, because you knew the church needed her leadership skills.

You think about your ordination service and the great expecta-tions you had about being part of something holy. You wanted to be a deacon because you longed to serve Christ in new, meaningful ways. But, as time passes, the big possibilities seem to grow much smaller. You wonder if this is all that God has in mind for the church—and for you.

The gap we feel from time to time between who we are and who we need to be is a wonderful gift from God. When we discover this gap and want to bridge it, we begin a conversation that can change us. "Who do we need to be?" doesn't have to undermine all of the answers we give to "Who are you?"—though it might cause us to rethink some of them. This question is weighty, so wrestling with it takes time and effort. Like Jacob's all-night match with the angel, such an effort will likely cost us something. We may need to let something go in order to reach for something else. The learning process may challenge us or test our limits. But such wrestling is also life giving. Catching a vision of who God wants us to become means imagining the future, finding new direction, and dreaming new dreams.

"Who do we need to be?" is both a personal question and one the church needs to ponder. If our answers come too quickly or automatically, we have not understood what the question is asking. "Who do we need to be?" is a question we have to live with. When we do so, it shapes us. It becomes part of our prayer and our worship. "Who do we need to be?" is a question we need God's help to answer. God seems to delight in this kind of conversation.

# Part of God's Masterpiece

Have you seen "living masterpieces" that bring classic paintings to life by recreating them with real, extremely still people? I don't know anyone who became *Mona Lisa* or the guy with the pitchfork in *American Gothic*, but I would love to see someone I know step into one of these staged pictures. With the right costumes, make-up, and setting, actors become amazing reproductions. When people who know the actors well look at them closely, they still recognize the person they love. They just see that person in a remarkably new way.

The church is well acquainted with the concept behind this picture show. The Creator we serve is always inviting us to step into the divine Artist's creation and become part of a living masterpiece. God wants us to find our place in the classic stories of Scripture and show the world how such truths come alive. So we step into the disciples' sandals and discover how challenging and life-changing it is to follow Jesus; we run home as the repentant son does and receive his father's forgiving embrace; we sit at Jesus' feet like Mary does, and choose Christ's better way. When we step inside God's story, we discover how much we resemble the characters there. The experience helps us see ourselves differently and find new ways to be part of the Artist's work.

God is an Artist, and we are the material with which God works. Paul writes in Ephesians 2:10 (NRSV), "For we are what he has made us, created in Christ Jesus for good works, which God prepared beforehand to be our way of life." Other translations call us God's creation, handiwork, masterpiece, and accomplishment. They translate this from the Greek word *poima*, the root of our word "poem." Imagine your life as a poem that God keeps working on. Throughout Scripture, God continues creating new ways to relate to us when we fail to be faithful. God writes on our hearts; God creates a new covenant; God loves and forgives; God sends the Spirit. Our Creator cares about relating to us and invests in this relationship. God has ideas, plans, and artistic visions that are waiting to be tried in us, with us, and through us. How do we recognize and value the living masterpieces that God will use us to create?

Living masterpieces are God's specialty. "For it was you who formed my inward parts; you knit me together in my mother's womb," sings the psalmist. "I praise you, for I am fearfully and wonderfully made. Wonderful are your works; that I know very well" (Ps 139:13-14). From the beginning, God has invited everyone to share in the joy of the creative process:

So God created humankind in his image, in the image of God he created them; male and female he created them. God blessed them, and God said to them, "Be fruitful and multiply; and fill the earth and subdue it; and have dominion over the fish of the sea and over the birds of the air and over every living thing that moves upon the earth." (Gen 1:27-28)

Jesus became God's living masterpiece, picturing what love and forgiveness look like. Then Jesus began inspiring other living pictures of service and care. In the Gospels, he often uses the word *diakonos,* as well as other related terms referring to deacons, to describe the way we need to act. The basic meaning of this word in secular Greek is "servant," or one engaged in menial tasks, particularly food service. Jesus illustrated what these words meant with his own servanthood, which gave them new significance. When the first deacons are called in Acts 6, Luke uses the word *diakonos* for them, linking this new office of serving the neglected to the act of serving Christ by continuing the focus of Jesus' ministry. The first deacons step into the living masterpiece Jesus created and find their place in it.

"Only in Jesus [do] we learn what *diakonia* really is," T. F. Torrance writes. "For this reason the Early Church saw delineated in the deacon's office more than anywhere else the likeness of Jesus, the servant of the Lord."[1] Torrance tells us that today's church needs "a massive recovery of authentic *diakonia*" if we want the world to see a living picture of Christ and if we want to "minister the mercy of God to the needs of [people] in the deep root of their evil and in the real sting of their misery."[2]

Over the course of church history, the role and form of deacon ministry has changed, but the purpose for which God created deacons—to extend Christ's ministry into the world while giving the world a picture of Christ as it does so—remains essential for the church. When the first deacons served the Hellenist widows in

Acts 6, they were not simply easing tensions and saving time for the apostles. Early deacons understood that they were serving as a picture of Christ, representing the Suffering Servant by identifying with the suffering, the poor, and the marginalized.

Through our relationship with Christ, deacons find the strength, encouragement, and love they need to minister in difficult circumstances. Edward Buelt writes that deacons who allow their joy for ministry to die cannot represent Christ in a luminous way. "For this joy to develop in a deep and spiritually profound fashion," Buelt advises us to focus on continual formation.[3]

From its earliest beginnings, the church had a Christ-centered understanding of service that recognized

> Christ Himself . . . is personally—though hiddenly and mysteriously—present in the needy, which makes it impossible for the believing Church ever to regard or treat them as merely so many cases of poverty, malnutrition or disease. For others they may perhaps be a problem to be solved, a political, social or economic untidiness to be cleared up, a potential danger to be neutralized: for the Christian Church they must always remain persons, whose status as persons is guaranteed by the mystery disclosed in Matthew 25:33ff.[4]

Who do deacons need to be? Be people who are aware of the ways God is working in us and through us. Be people who are ready to join Christ in whatever living pictures of service he invites us to step into. Be good stewards who joyfully share the gifts we find in our relationship with God with those who need our care.

# Individual Exercises

1. Reflecting on Psalm 139:13-14 and Ephesians 2:10, how can you recognize and celebrate the living portrait that you are today? Give some examples.

2. What do you think others saw in you when they elected you as a deacon?

3. If you are one of God's unfinished portraits, what do you think God might want to add to the portrait?

4. Name three events that have been faith-defining for you as an adult.

# Group Conversation

1. Relate some insight, experience, or event you recorded in the individual exercises from this session.

2. Is our church a place where we really know one another? If not, how can we change that?

3. In the parable of the nominating committee, there are two contrasting questions: "Who needs to be a deacon?" and "Who do deacons need to be?" What do these two questions mean, and how important are they for your diaconate and church?

4. Who have been deacon role models for you?

# Deacons Are Beloved Children of God Who Experience Grace

## A Parable: Luke 15:11-24

(11) Then Jesus said, "There was a man who had two sons. (12) The younger of them said to his father, 'Father, give me the share of the property that will belong to me.' So he divided his property between them. (13) A few days later the younger son gathered all he had and traveled to a distant country, and there he squandered his property in dissolute living. (14) When he had spent everything, a severe famine took place throughout that country, and he began to be in need. (15) So he went and hired himself out to one of the citizens of that country, who sent him to his fields to feed the pigs. (16) He would gladly have filled himself with the pods that the pigs were eating; and no one gave him anything. (17) But when he came to himself he said, 'How many of my father's hired hands have bread enough and to spare, but here I am dying of hunger! (18) I will get up and go to my father, and I will say to him, "Father, I have sinned against heaven and before you; (19) I am no longer worthy to be called your son; treat me like one of your hired hands."' (20) So

he set off and went to his father. But while he was still far off, his father saw him and was filled with compassion; he ran and put his arms around him and kissed him. (21) Then the son said to him, 'Father, I have sinned against heaven and before you; I am no longer worthy to be called your son.' (22) But the father said to his slaves, 'Quickly, bring out a robe—the best one—and put it on him; put a ring on his finger and sandals on his feet. (23) And get the fatted calf and kill it, and let us eat and celebrate; (24) for this son of mine was dead and is alive again; he was lost and is found!' And they began to celebrate."

We always need God's grace to become the people we need to be. Becoming the kinds of deacons that God envisions is not a do-it-ourselves project. Thankfully, God is with us when we finally recognize our limitations, shortcomings, and sin so that we can see the hope, forgiveness, and reconciliation that are also present. Through his story about the prodigal son, his older brother, and the father who longs to love them both, Jesus invites us to step inside the parable and make the younger son's journey from repentance to reconciliation our own experience. Traveling the path between where we are and where we need to be means passing through honest moments of the soul where we confess we are lost and need direction.

You may not see yourself as the prodigal type; the five adjectives you use to describe yourself might be antonyms for the younger son, and vice versa. Yet whether we realize it or not, God is always waiting for us to step into the living masterpiece that Jesus created and take our place as the younger son. While this may humiliate the firstborns and chronically responsible among us, it helps us find our way home and leads us to the relationship with God that we long for most. When we confess and own the prodigal in ourselves, we experience the truth of the gospel.

Our "loose living" may not mirror what Jesus pictures as the younger son's way to waste his inheritance. We may consider frugality a virtue. We may be careful in ways that the Pharisees, to whom Jesus tells this story, would appreciate. But Jesus wants us all to recognize our family resemblance to the self-determined spendthrift. Even those of us who cautiously guard our reputations have different forms of loose living that will lead us into the far country. After all, even the short distance between the field where the older brother works and the party at the house that the father pleads with his eldest to join seems to be a walk too lengthy for the indignant son.

Maybe we live loosely by squandering the time and opportunities we have to become the people God wants us to be. Maybe we throw away valuable relationships by letting minor matters get in the way. Perhaps hearing Christ's message and walking away from what it calls us to be is our loose living of choice. When Jesus invites us to love the Lord with all we are, and love our neighbors as we love ourselves, and we constantly find ways to politely decline, aren't we squandering our inheritance in loose living?

The opening words of Luke 15:17 mark the moment that we all experience on the way to becoming who we need to be: *when he came to himself.* We sometimes talk about the fact that not all of us have conversion experiences as dramatic as Paul's was on the Damascus road. Those of us who were nurtured in the church since cradle roll may not remember a time when we didn't know about Christ. But this does not mean we can bypass the moment of seeing ourselves clearly in the light of God's love and grace.

As a youth, I often wondered what God looked like and what I should picture when I closed my eyes to pray. Then one day, when my need for God seemed intense, instead of thinking about what God looked like, I thought about how I appeared to God. As I prayed, I grew aware of the many masks I wear, even during prayer, when I am praying to the One who created me and knows who I am without all of my facades. With God's help, prayer that day became a process of peeling off one mask after another and recognizing who I was underneath them all. When I read about the moment when the prodigal *came to himself,* I remember how that feels.

After the younger son sees himself more clearly, he knows his life must change. He knows he needs to return to his father. On the long walk home, he practices his confession and how he will seek repentance for what he did. The distance in their relationship seems almost insurmountable, so when he sees his dad running towards him, bridging the gap between them with an astounding embrace, the prodigal is overwhelmed by the grace of it all. The father holds nothing back as he restores his wayward child, giving him all that he needs to become who he was meant to be.

When has this son's experience been yours?

On the night of my grandfather's funeral, we stayed up late in the beloved house my grandparents shared. That night, as I caught up with family in those vulnerable hours of a deep loss when we talk about what matters most, I thought about where I was in my life—as opposed to where I used to think I would be when I had to say good-bye to my granddad. I thought I would be farther along by that point. I thought I would have accomplished more. Time was passing so quickly. Wasn't I supposed to know more in my mid-thirties than I did before? Wasn't I supposed to have a clearer sense of direction by then? I imagined a map unfolded before me with one point labeled "who I am" and another marked "who I need to be." The distance between the two points felt immense. Any roadway between them seemed sketchy at best. While it was good to finally acknowledge the distance and realize where I needed to be, figuring out how to get there seemed like a challenge hard to overcome.

Our conversation slowed down and the house grew quiet. At the funeral, we told about the experience that everyone who had spent the night at our grandparents' home had shared. No matter how late it was, we always heard our grandparents reading

Scripture to each other before turning out their bedroom light. That night, when we realized how late it was, we braced ourselves for the sadness we expected to feel during the silence we expected to experience. Instead, we heard my grandmother reading Scripture in a firm voice. When she ended her verses, there was brief silence. Then we heard my aunt's voice as she finished reading the passage for the night. She stepped into what we pictured as an insurmountable gap and showed us the way forward.

The moments when we realize we have lost our direction and know we are not where we need to be are gifts of grace. They help us come to ourselves and realize that our lives must change. God meets us in the gap between who we are and who we need to be and leads us home. Churches shaped by Christ's story help us discover what it means for this story to shape us as well.

# Individual Exercise

In reflecting on your experience of grace as a beloved child of God, compose your spiritual autobiography with honesty as your goal. Consider these questions as you write your story, perhaps in a spiritual journal:

- What role did your parents and other adult caregivers play in shaping your worldview, sense of security, and view of God?
- Looking back, can you identify other adults whom you now believe God sent your way?
- Where and how did you first hear or learn about God?
- What helped or hindered your acceptance of God's love and direction?
- How did you become a Christ follower?
- What have been the good things about your journey with Christ? What have been the challenges?
- How have you managed to stick with Christ?

Take a good look at the total story of your life, look to see where God showed up along the way, and frame the story in a way that you can remember and share.

In composing your spiritual autobiography, the following experiences from the writers of this resource may inspire you.

### A Brief Spiritual Autobiography (Mike Smith)

I was in my late twenties before I realized my entire childhood and adolescence taught me not to trust others. As a child of a practicing alcoholic, I learned not to trust even my own family and to keep my distance from anything that looked remotely like intimacy.

I grew up in a time when our culture was obsessed with what we called "the Communist menace." My high school and college years were dominated by the height of the Vietnam conflict and the shattering revelation that government officials might lie to us (i.e., Lyndon Johnson and his administration with reference to Vietnam, and Richard Nixon with reference to his involvement in the Watergate scandal).

What about church? The truth is that my church preached about Christ and the way of love, even as it consistently embraced and practiced the quiet racism characteristic of my rural community.

Looking back, I now see that my family, social, and church contexts conditioned me to be distrustful, to be hesitant to risk trusting anyone or any institution.

To put it mildly, trusting God did not come easily to me. Even today, trusting God requires work on my part. That I can trust God is a bit of a miracle, a miracle brought to pass in large part by some people God sent my way over the years and the ways in which they countered the trust-destroying factors in my life. Several teachers played important roles, mostly by consistently demonstrating a concern for my well-being and following through on commitments they made.

The turning point came my first year in college, when I met the woman who one day would become my wife. She came from a family situation even more difficult than mine, yet she seemed able to extend trust to others and especially to God. Over time, as I learned to trust her and saw more of her ability to trust, I started to believe trust was a way of life worth exploring. I embarked on a decade-long journey that led me to confront the roots of my inability to trust and shaped my sense of pastoral vocation.

Now, when I read the Scriptures I tend to see them as the story of God's unending attempt to help us choose to trust God and build a trustworthy and trusting community. For example, Paul's call for us to work out our salvation with fear and trembling resonates with me. God freely offers me God's trust through Christ. My personal history is the story of my learning to accept such a gift, hold on to my awareness of it, and remodel my life so that I treat others as God treats me.

## A Memory of Deacons (Guy Sayles)

When I was in elementary school, my family was very active in the First Baptist Church of Conley, Georgia (a few miles south of Atlanta). The church was a haven and second home for me, and its people were my extended family. Many of the adults were my unofficially adopted "aunts" and "uncles"; sometimes, I heard people call each other "brother" and "sister." In that extended family, we saw the church's deacons as role models or, as the title of this resource put it, exemplars. When the church elected them, the focus was on their character and Christ-likeness, their knowledge and wisdom, and their commitment and faithfulness to the ministry of the congregation.

We knew deacons weren't perfect, but we also trusted that they were serious about following Jesus and doing what was best for the church. My impression then was that the church was saying about deacons, "Here's what a Christian looks like"; "In this family (the church), these are the ways we live"; and "Do what you see them do." They led us not so much by the decisions they made but by the example they offered. That example was most visible, of course, in what they did. I think that congregations still look to deacons, whatever their specific roles and responsibilities in the church, to be role models and examples. It is both an honor and a responsibility.

## A Discovery of Prayer (Daniel Vestal)

I grew up in an evangelical tradition where the emphasis of prayer was talking to God, but there is another side of prayer. God wants me to listen. God wants to speak, commune, and communicate with me. What God wants to communicate most of all is how great God's love and grace is toward me.

This discovery introduced me to the practice of contemplative prayer, or listening prayer. It set me on a journey and introduced me to some pioneers of prayer who became my mentors and teachers. Some of these mentors were alien to my faith tradition. But I learned from them how important it is to listen to God. I am still learning how to release to God my competitiveness and my need to be in control. I am still learning to surrender to God my anxieties, my addictions, my ambitions and to abandon my temper and tongue to God. I struggle still with compulsions and a performance-based religion, and I'm still tempted to measure my worth by what I achieve, accumulate, or accomplish. Slowly and painfully, I have been learning how much God loves me, treasures me, and values me. This creates an incredible freedom and joy that brings forth love both for God and for people. The result is prayer.

# My Spiritual Autobiography

# Group Conversation

1. What do you have in common with the prodigal son? When have you experienced the far country? When have you squandered your inheritance of life and other gifts that God has given you?

2. When have you experienced that moment of "coming to yourself," when you saw who you are most clearly and realized your need for God?

3. Consider sharing your spiritual autobiography with the group.

4. If you feel comfortable, share a faith-defining event from your life with the group.

# Deacons Are Members of Christ's Church Who Are Filled with the Spirit

## A Parable: Luke 15:25-32

(25) "Meanwhile, the older son was in the field. When he came near the house, he heard music and dancing. (26) So he called one of the servants and asked him what was going on. (27) 'Your brother has come,' he replied, 'and your father has killed the fattened calf because he has him back safe and sound.' (28) The older brother became angry and refused to go in. So his father went out and pleaded with him. (29) But he answered his father, 'Look! All these years I've been slaving for you and never disobeyed your orders. Yet you never gave me even a young goat so I could celebrate with my friends. (30) But when this son of yours who has squandered your property with prostitutes comes home, you kill the fattened calf for him!' (31) 'My son,' the father said, 'you are always with me, and everything I have is yours. (32) But we had to celebrate and be glad, because this brother of yours was dead and is alive again; he was lost and is found.'"

This story of the loving father shows us who we need to be as individuals and as the community of God's family. By telling *this* story to religious people who used their faith as a tool to distance themselves from others, Jesus is trying to correct their mistaken perspective. God's love, Jesus teaches us all, overcomes the differences that divide us. Around God's banquet table are a multitude of different opinions, religious perspectives, work ethics, and personality types. Jesus seems to say that participating in the father's party, and discovering that the people there are our brothers and sisters, matters more than the obstacles that threaten to separate us. Jesus wants us to see that any child of God is our sister or brother. These relationships are some of God's best gifts to us. God creates a community in which we can give, receive, and become who we were meant to be.

When the younger son returns, the loving father is ready to get the party started. The older son cannot envision what his father clearly sees: a welcome-home celebration for the prodigal is a party for all of them, for all members of the family. The party is for us all. Without the elder brother, the experience is incomplete. This event is a gift that the father wants his oldest son to open. It is meant for the hard worker as well as for the child who lost his way. If the eldest refuses to accept the party invitation, the father knows that the party is incomplete. Not only was his youngest son lost; his oldest is lost also. The father pleads for him to enter the festivities because the father knows that this is not a gala to reward irresponsible behavior. This abundant gift is a catalyst for a new family dynamic. This party begins a new day of possibility where participants move beyond their pasts into God's future and focus on opening the best gifts.

What keeps us from saying yes to this party that Jesus pleads with us to join? What keeps our churches from being banquet halls for God's kind of celebration? Perhaps Jesus leaves his story open-ended so we will consider how we will respond. Will the older son go with his father and pick up a plate of barbecue, or will he stay out in the field and sulk? Will this encounter with his dad lead to his own "coming to himself" moment that he so desperately needs? Does he ever recognize that he is lost in the far country, too? Does he glimpse the better possibility of who he could become? Does he ever understand what his father knows or glimpse what his father sees?

Surely the Pharisees, after hearing about this brilliant invitation to join the party, caught the meaning of Jesus' message, even if they refused it. A relationship with God includes a relationship with God's people. Loving God means loving neighbor. To belong to Christ is to become part of Christ's people, baptized into Christ's church. We are members of Christ's body, sharing one Lord, one faith, and one baptism. Christ's vision for the church is a masterpiece that God pleads with us to join. As Paul wrote to the Corinthian church that was characterized by its many divisions, "Christ is just like the human body—a body is a unit and has many parts; and all the parts of the body are one body, even though there are many. We were all baptized by one Spirit into one body, whether Jew or Greek, or slave or free, and we were given one Spirit to drink" (1 Cor 12:12-13). Those who refuse this gift by clinging to judgmental lives not only miss the party but also they miss its purpose.

When are we slow to join Christ's party? When do we spend more time arguing over the guest list than we spend getting to know the people Christ welcomes to the table? What was problematic for the elder brother has been problematic for the church since its earliest days. We forget, or overlook, the fact that being invited is God's great gift to *us*, the centerpiece of all presents. We start thinking of God's gift as *ours*—*our* party, *our* church—when all of it belongs to God. Like the older son, we want to believe that it is our right to determine whose name is on the guest list and who has earned the father's love. We forget that if we only receive what we rightfully earn, our lives will be so much smaller, so much less, than they will if we receive the life that God's grace creates for us. When we glimpse the grace that can save and restore us, and we see ourselves in its light—for the first time or the fiftieth—we can't help thanking God for inviting us, and everyone else, to this party. And then entering it fully is our best response.

Recognizing that grace is what brings us to God's party transforms our attitude. "Because of the grace that God gave me," Paul wrote, "I can say to each one of you: don't think of yourself more highly than you ought to think" (Rom 12:3a). Humility is a mark of authentic faith. Think about the times in Scripture when someone encounters God's holiness and responds with humility. Remember how Isaiah discovers God in the temple and suddenly realizes his own unworthiness. Consider Simon Peter's experience in Luke 5. After Jesus tells the veteran fisherman how to catch fish, Simon initially replies, "Master, we've worked hard all night and caught nothing. But because you say so, I'll drop the nets" (Luke 5:5). What is the tone in his voice? Is there a hint of self-righteousness in it? Perhaps Simon is also thinking that fishermen know more about getting a good catch than carpenters. Maybe this is why Simon Peter reacts to the result of Jesus' fishing lesson with utter humility, saying, "Leave me, Lord, for I'm a sinner!"

We need to step into this story and take our place with Simon. We too have areas of expertise where we think we know at least almost everything about what works and what doesn't. Deacons and other leaders in ministry do know a great deal about how churches work much of the time. We've spent our time in the field. We've invested the 10,000 hours of practicing church that Malcolm Gladwell says it takes to become a master in something. Like Simon, however, we need to remember that we never outgrow our need to learn from God. Humility surrounds the holy experiences that we urgently need.

If biblical characters who encounter God learn to respond with humility, how do communities who encounter God react? It makes sense that when churches encounter God in the moments of their work and worship, arrogance will disappear. The humility that results from encounters with Christ makes it possible for churches to deepen and grow. The vulnerability and humility that come when arrogance leaves make room for every member to be loved and valued, no matter what their contribution might be. Our initial experience of encountering Christ is the first of many gifts God will give.

Just as younger brothers need moments when they "come to themselves" and recognize the gap between who they are and who they need to be, churches need those moments. Sometimes through humbling circumstances, churches discover newfound humility that helps them experience God's grace and forgiveness.

When has your community "come to itself" and re-experienced the joy of being the body of Christ? What difference has a humbling moment made in the ongoing life of your congregation? How might newfound humility make your deacons more aware of and open to learning from God?

When I was a young minister, I had big dreams for our small-town youth group. Then I learned that our teenagers didn't like each other much. The fellowships we planned always felt forced. Bible studies ended without drawing the group closer. Friendships among the youth never seemed to take. We finally decided to spend one summer making day trips to Louisville, our nearest city, to help various inner-city ministers do their work. The leaders who were immersed in their ministries talked to us about what being Christ's church in the world means. They gave our youth tasks that would help them share in the church's work. Our group served in new ways.

As I drove the teenagers home after the last long day of our summer-long project, I was amazed by the conversations going on in the seats behind me. The youth who were once resistant to building community with each other were planning their own get-together for the next day. Hadn't we seen each other enough that week? As they were learning to serve together, they were also learning to enjoy and appreciate each other. As they worked together, they discovered that joy and celebration were gifts Christ included in that experience.

When has serving as the body of Christ transformed your deacons? When you think about who deacons need to be, what ministries and mission come to mind? What would it take to nurture the gift of humility in your deacon group and in your church? How would pursuing such activities help your church grow in Christ?

## Gifted with the Spirit

Step into the prodigal's story just after his father runs to embrace him. The son begins to give the speech he has practiced on his long walk home, a speech full of repentance. Before he can offer his plans for penance, the father interrupts. What seems most urgent to this forgiving parent is making sure that his child is equipped with the best gifts he can give him. The son receives the finest robe, a ring that says he belongs, and sandals the feel of which he'd almost forgotten. With these gifts, the father restores and redeems his relationship with his son. The father immediately orders a feast for the occasion to celebrate this new life.

The parents among us, who wonder what they need to learn about parenting from this father, may question his extravagant gift giving. Isn't the father's forgiveness gift enough? Why is this parent so quick to give such great presents to a son who certainly has done nothing to deserve them? Couldn't he at least wait to see if the son follows through with his newfound love for his family? Maybe he could give his child the robe the next night, if he shows up for work the next morning and does his fair share in the fields.

What becomes most clear in this gift-giving moment of the story is that the father's overwhelming love is central to the parable. The abundant love for his children that fills this parent's heart and character is almost unimaginable. The gift of this love cannot be contained or limited. It expresses itself in a variety of ways. God always comes bearing gifts—gifts God creates, gifts of relationship with us and with others, gifts of forgiveness and restoration, the gift of new covenants when the old ones need updating, the gift of Jesus, the gift of God's Spirit, and the gifts the Spirit gives to each member of Christ's church to use for the common good. God enjoys giving and wants us to enjoy it as well. It's no wonder, considering how often Scripture pictures God's kingdom as a party or a banquet.

Our relationship with God is itself a life-changing gift. Receiving God's love makes us gifted in ways we did not earn or achieve. Like the robe-draped, ring-bearing, sandal-wearing son, God leads us into a family celebration and makes us welcome there. We have a place at the table, a people to be part of, and a purpose to pursue. We share in God's work, God's vision, and God's hope. We become part of God's love, and we learn to love.

This loving father's story is the masterpiece God invites us to step into. The invitation to find our place in it is a great gift, an amazing picture of who we need to be. God opens the door to the celebration and urges us to come inside.

A huge part of the joy of being the church together comes when we discover the gifts that God gives our faith communities. Unfortunately, we don't always take the time we need to find, open, and explore these gifts. If you've ever unwrapped a present that you never took out of its box, you understand that this happens. Do we ever receive new members into our congregations but not recognize or use the gifts they bring with them? If you've ever received a gift that is capable of doing much more than you used it for, you recognize how churches can fail to fully appreciate and engage their members' gifts.

Now consider your congregation. What gifts has God given to your members that the church has never unwrapped? What possibilities could God be waiting for you to explore? When we celebrate the gifts God places among us, our life together becomes a gift itself, full of meaning and purpose. Such gift-opening moments form us and make Christ's mission more possible. God does not send anyone into the body of Christ empty-handed. Each of us has something God gave us to use for the common good.

How do we discover and nurture these gifts? How do we encourage their development? How do we see the potential that God has created for us? How do we become more gifted churches?

Sometimes we uncover the gifts God gives us when we discover a need God wants us to meet. Remember that deacons were first created in Acts 6 to address a tension that was developing in the early church. By serving the neglected Hellenist widows, deacons became the means God used to stretch and fulfill the church's mission.

Deacons have the same calling today to further God's mission just as the first deacons did. Deacons know where the church is needed outside its walls. Deacon service takes many forms as it reaches out to serve God's mission. When churches recognize, bless, support, and claim the daily ministry that happens through the spiritual gifts of its deacons and church members—in elementary schools, group homes, foster parent meetings, pro bono work, hospitals, and nursing homes—the mission of the body of Christ grows stronger.

The Spirit gives our churches the gifts we need. We may need to learn how to recognize them. Gift-giving is a key to God's vision for the church. Exercising gifts is essential for our spiritual growth. Ephesians 4:7-16 is one of several passages in Paul's letters where he emphasizes how crucial gifts are: "God has given his grace to each one of us measured out by the gift that is given by Christ" (v. 7). "His purpose was to equip God's people for the work of serving and building up the body of Christ until we all reach the unity of faith and knowledge of God's Son. God's goal is for us to become mature adults—to be fully grown, measured by the standard of the fullness of Christ" (vv. 12-13). How might we discover and nurture the gifts around us? Could you develop ministry teams that form around your members' gifts for service? If you already do this, what new teams might be needed? What gifts has God given to your church that some are longing to use, and others need to receive? How could the church take God's vision for using our gifts more seriously? How could we create new avenues within existing ministries, or create new ministries altogether so that everyone has a way to serve Christ using their gifts?

How could we cultivate a gift-giving culture in our churches that would reflect our gift-giving God? How could we better identify, call out, nurture, and encourage gifts in our congregations? How do we make this part of our work in every area of church life—from involving children in opportunities to serve to making sure that the elderly have ways to exercise their purpose?

In her book *Eighth Day of Creation*, Elizabeth O'Connor, who belonged to the Church of the Saviour in Washington, DC, emphasizes why the church felt that it was crucial for everyone in their congregation to find a place to exercise their gifts. She draws on Dietrich Bonhoeffer's warning that communities that allow unemployed members will wither and die because of them. All members of Christ's body are gifted for and need definite tasks to perform so that they may realize they are an integral part of the community. Gordon Cosby, a founder of The Church of the Savior, preached that Paul's teachings about spiritual gifts contain "spiritual dynamite. If we will take them seriously, they will set off a revolution in the churches that will bring in a whole new age of the Spirit."[5]

If we could take a picture of our spiritual life right now and place it next to the masterpiece that God invites us to step into, how would they compare? What are the gifts that God has placed in your life? What are you bringing to the party that is God's kingdom? Maybe we see parts of the picture we never noticed before—a talent someone else is holding that we didn't know the person had. Maybe we find ourselves hesitant, unsure of where God's invitation will lead.

The good news is that the Artist is at work in us and in our churches. Notice the way God is building a characteristic here and adding another gift there. God's Spirit will lead us, helping us become who we need to be.

# Individual Exercises

1. What do you have in common with the older brother? When have you refused to be reconciled with someone Jesus wants you to celebrate? When are you slow to join Christ's party?

2. What does humility look like in the church? What impact does it have on us and on the world? How could we nurture it and experience it? Why should we do so?

3. When has humbly serving as the body of Christ transformed you and your deacons? What ministries and missions create this kind of humility—and transformation?

4. Is there a difference between natural talents and spiritual gifts that God gives to each of us?

# Group Conversation

1. The parable of Jesus in Luke 15 gives us a glimpse of God as a loving Father with two different sons. What does this parable teach us about the nature of the church?

2. Compose a brief story of your church and give attention to decisions and actions that have shaped its witness.

3. Discuss the character and composition, life and ministry of your church in light of the teachings of the parable of the prodigal son.

4. The Holy Spirit is given to each member of Christ's church. What would happen in our church if we all recognized that gift in ourselves and in others?

5. How effectively does our church help each member discover and use their spiritual gifts in ministry? Explore the meaning of "giftedness" for the church.

# What Do Deacons Need to Know?

The second question has to do with faith development and the more cognitive side of Christian discipleship. Faith has an object. Faith has content. So knowing requires learning and understanding. We are commanded to love God with our minds, and we are promised that "the truth will set us free" (John 8:32). Those who follow Jesus are called "disciples," which means we are "learners."

## Session 4: Deacons Know the Scripture and How to Interpret It in the Light of Jesus

This session inspires conversation about the importance and nature of Scripture. It doesn't assume that deacons understand the meta-narrative contained in Scripture, the history of the canon, or the methods of interpretation. The individual exercises and group questions invite deacons to enter into thoughtful study and reflection, and then interpret two New Testament texts based on what they actually know.

## Session 5: Deacons Learn Church History

This session inspires conversation about the Christian story beyond one's personal experience and local congregation. It introduces church history by offering seven "snapshots" and gives a broad overview that illustrates the richness of the Christian story and diverse ways that story influences us today. The individual exercises and group conversation challenge deacons to broaden and deepen their understanding beyond the present.

### Session 6: Deacons Think Theologically

This session inspires conversation about theology and theological thinking. It offers a "primer" on theology from a pastoral and practical perspective, challenging deacons to examine their theological prejudices and presuppositions as well as prevailing theological notions around us. The individual exercises and the group conversation questions aim at theological thinking that is centered in Christ.

# Deacons Know the Scripture and How to Interpret It in Light of Jesus

Scholars debate whether Stephen should be labeled a deacon, but in my experience nearly all modern church members think of Stephen and his six fellow servants as the first deacons. The church in Jerusalem selected them to ensure fairness in the daily distribution of food to widows (Acts 6:1-6). Some of them, such as Stephen and Philip, soon took on other tasks as well.

Philip may have been the first disciple to share the gospel with and baptize a Gentile, the Ethiopian eunuch (Acts 8:26-40). The story reveals the role knowledge plays in their conversation. The eunuch is reading the prophet Isaiah. Prompted by the Spirit, Philip asks the man if he understands the text, and the Ethiopian replies, "How can I, unless someone guides me?" Philip makes use of the Old Testament Scriptures, interpreting them in light of Jesus. In response, the eunuch asks if there is anything to hinder him from being baptized. Philip then baptizes the man.

Stephen becomes the first Christian martyr (Acts 6:8-60). Accused of blasphemy against Moses and God, Stephen is brought before the council of elders and scribes (most likely the Sanhedrin). When the high priest asks Stephen if the accusations are true, Stephen responds with one of the most remarkable speeches recorded in the Scriptures. Read Acts 6 for yourself, and I think you will notice how Stephen draws on a wealth of knowledge. He reviews in brief the history of Israel, from the calling of Abraham to the building of the first temple. Stephen concludes by citing Isaiah 66:1-2 in order to drive home two points: God does not dwell in houses made of human hands, and God's people have a history of resisting the work of God's Spirit, including God's work through the prophets and the Messiah.

The story ends in violence, as Stephen is dragged outside the city and stoned to death. For our purposes, take special note of how Stephen possesses an impressive command of history and the Scriptures. He not only makes use of such knowledge but also dares to undertake the theological task of reinterpreting both the Scriptures and history in light of Jesus.

We may or may not be called upon to minister in the dramatic fashion of Philip or Stephen, but we must learn from their example. Deacons minister best when they come to know the Scriptures, the history of God's people, and how to interpret all things in light of Jesus Christ.

As we've seen, Stephen interpreted the Hebrew Bible and the history of Israel from the perspective of an overarching story. He took the various stories found in his Scriptures and reinterpreted them in light of a larger story.

Nowadays, we often call such a larger storyline a meta-narrative. The concept is not new. Jesus used a meta-narrative to reinterpret the Law. While he asserted that not a single element in the law would be lost or cast aside, he also exercised enormous creativity and authority in dealing with the Scriptures. Some of the most

shocking words Jesus uttered were, "You have heard that it was said
. . . but I say to you." Read Matthew 5:17-48, and you'll start to
appreciate how Jesus held the Scriptures (the Old Testament) in
high esteem yet also interpreted them in ways that scandalized his
listeners. No doubt, Jesus felt free to do so in his capacity as the
Messiah, but it's also clear that he made use of a meta-narrative.

What was this meta-narrative? The four Gospels offer clues
as they share how Jesus depicts God and humanity. Jesus pictures
God as a loving parent whose children test God in various ways:
by fleeing God, trying to take over God's farmhouse and exclude
erring brothers from it, wandering off like silly sheep, attempting
to claim God's vineyard as their own, getting lost in the delusion
of self-righteous forms of religion, and the like. God, according to
Jesus, desires all God's children to trust God, come home to God,
make room for one another, and be good neighbors to all. When
Jesus deals with a selection from the Old Testament Scriptures, he
does so in light of such an overarching story.

Deacons help others deal best with the Bible when deacons
know and use a Christ-honoring meta-narrative to interpret the
Scriptures. Hopefully, the larger narrative we use will bear a close
resemblance to the one used by Jesus.

Don't expect all deacons to use the same words. My third grade
teacher often said, "Until you can put something into your own
words, you don't understand it. When you finally cast something
in your own words, you own it. It becomes part of you." She was
right.

Try writing your own version of a Christ-honoring meta-narrative by which to evaluate and interpret all Scriptures. Share the
results with your fellow deacons, and learn from one another. Don't
be surprised when you hear someone else's words and think, "Now
that's what I was trying to say."

To help you get started, I'll share the meta-narrative I've used
in recent years. It goes as follows.

*God created the world and called it good, by which God meant the world was set up just as it should be to launch a long, long story—a story that would unfold in God-honoring ways and enrich all of creation. God created humanity as free beings, humans whom he called and invited to follow God, know God, partner well with God, and love God, one another, and the world.*

*Humanity, though, proved unwilling to accept the gift God offered. Almost from our beginnings, we sought to walk separate from God. This did not work out well for us or for the world.*

*Finally, God initiated a long-term project designed to recreate us. Starting with Abraham and Sarah and working with their descendants, God created a people who could at least dream of a new kind of human community—a community that seeks to know and trust God, offers meaningful liberation to all, produces a society in which even the powerless are safe, and lives toward a day when God's presence might be directly experienced and embraced.*

*God stayed faithful to God's dream over the centuries, even when the people pushed back. God worked through some of them, especially the prophets and even an occasional ruler, to remind them of God's purpose and hope for them. And over the course of time, just when it looked as if the community might be swallowed up by history, God brought forth the one person in whom God's dream was fully realized: the Messiah, the one named Jesus.*

*The Jesus story, told from various perspectives by the four Gospels, is the tale of God's willingness to enter directly into the messy world of humanity and make a home among us. The Jesus story declares that those who enter into his life will find that God's way is a real option in the world as we know it, not simply a nice idea or something reserved for heaven. Jesus opens the way for any of us to step into the Jesus life.*

*The rest of the New Testament is the story of the struggles, failures, and successes of the first generation of Christ followers, as they tried to step into the life of Jesus.*

You might say there's not much to this, but it's a meta-narrative cast in my own words, one that enables me to help others deal with passages drawn from nearly all parts of the Bible. The longer I live with an overarching story in which Jesus is the center of the Bible's story—the one toward whom it moves, the one from whom it extends into the entire world, and the one in whom the particulars of Scripture find their God-honoring meaning—the more convinced I am of the necessity of a meta-narrative.

Charles Spurgeon, the famous English Baptist minister of the eighteenth century, is reputed to have said words to this effect: "I start with a Scripture and go straight to Jesus." My approach might be described as follows: "I start with Jesus and go from him to the rest of the Scriptures."

# Formation of the Biblical Canon

As Christians, we trust that God inspired the writers of Scripture. How did such inspiration work, and how did the various books and letters and other forms of literature come together to make what we call "the Bible"? Followers of Jesus, who believe in the Incarnation, should not be surprised that the answers lie in history. After all, if God chose to be revealed most directly and clearly through a particular human life lived within history, wouldn't God choose to employ a similar strategy for the development of the Scriptures? As it turns out, that's precisely what God did.

Start with a term: *canon*. The first time I heard this word used in a lecture, I immediately thought of military artillery. Shortly thereafter, I learned its actual meaning: rule or measure. The Bible is sometimes called the Christian canon because it consists of various writings that God's people found measured up to the task of Christian formation.

The history of the canon's development is long and complicated, but we can make the story part of our leadership toolbox by keeping in mind a few key matters.

First, the books, letters, poetry, and other forms of literature in the Bible were written at various times over the course of roughly one thousand years (from 900 BCE through 100 CE). Each author wrote from within a particular historical context. The meaning of words and phrases varied over the centuries. Even the concept of God grew. The Bible we use today might best be viewed as a library of the diverse ways in which God's people experienced, conceptualized, and dealt with God at various times and under a range of circumstances. We serve the church best when we acknowledge this is so and wrestle with the challenges presented by such diversity.

For example, portions of the Hebrew Bible depict God telling God's people to exterminate those they conquer. Jesus, on the other hand, insists that God's people must practice love toward all others, including enemies. Both commands are found within the covers of the Bible, and this raises a host of questions. Did God change God's mind, or did God's people misunderstand the original intent? Did Jesus describe God's intention for all times and places? Does the teaching of Jesus trump the command attributed to Moses? Must each generation of Christ followers confront the challenge of expanding their understanding of the universality of God's love? Such are the questions we confront when we take seriously the history of the Bible's development.

The more we know and understand the historical context of a given biblical author, the better prepared we are to deal with such questions. How might deacons learn more about the historical setting of each part of the Bible? The answers might affect the life of the deacon body, especially with regard to deacon orientation, group studies, retreats, and resources provided for personal study.

Second, the people of God decided which writings to include in the Bible. Mind you, Christians believe Holy Spirit worked in and through the historical process, but we sometimes are surprised to learn how the Spirit went about the task.

The first Christians regarded the Hebrew Bible or Old Testament (as Christians came to call it much later) as inspired Scripture. The Hebrew Bible achieved Scripture status over several centuries. By around 300 BCE, the Jews regarded the Pentateuch as Scripture. Many Jews accepted the Prophets (court histories, the Major Prophets, and the Minor Prophets) as Scripture by around 200 BCE. The Writings (the remainder of the Old Testament) probably enjoyed similar regard by 132 BCE. A council of rabbis meeting in Jamnia in 90 CE set the content of Hebrew Bible. From that time onward, most Jews accepted the council's decision as definitive.

The New Testament developed over the course of the first century CE as the letters of Paul, the four Gospels, and other writings began to circulate and be used among the churches. Most likely, first-century Christians did not treat such writings as Scripture per se. The more the items were used in worship and instruction alongside Old Testament Scriptures, the more they began to assume the air of Scripture.

By the middle of the second century, some Christians started to compose lists of writings they considered canonical. The content of the lists varied quite a bit. Marcion (around 144 CE) produced the earliest such list, in which he chose to drop the Old Testament while accepting Luke's Gospel and ten of Paul's letters as authoritative for the church. In reaction to Marcion, Christians in Rome developed their own canon (dating from somewhere between 170–200 CE). Their list of books suitable for worship and instruction included the four Gospels, Acts, thirteen of Paul's letters, the letters of John and Jude, and Revelation.

Churches and church leaders continued the trend over the next two or more centuries. In 325 CE, Eusebius of Caesarea included a list of universally accepted, disputed, and spurious Christian writings in his *Ecclesiastical History*. Under universally accepted writings, he listed the four Gospels, Acts, Paul's letters, Hebrews, 1 John, 1 Peter, and—with reservations—Revelation. Eusebius noted that other writings enjoyed wide usage, though a minority of the church rejected them: James, 2 Peter, 2 and 3 John, and Jude.

Eventually, two church councils affirmed the twenty-seven books and letters that make up our New Testament. The Council of Hippo, which met in 393 CE, and the Council of Carthage, which met in 397 CE, set the content of the New Testament. While not all Christians accepted the councils' decisions, most Christians have done so since the start of the fifth century CE.

The history of the canon's formation reminds us that God chooses to work in partnership with humans. Over the course of centuries, God prompted people to compose writings, test their usefulness in the context of worship and service, and decide which of them best served to shape them into individuals who might know, honor, and serve God.

# Interpreting Scripture

Many of us grew up hearing preachers proclaim, "The Bible says it. I believe it. That settles it." By now, I hope we realize that the task of biblical interpretation is a tad more complicated. If you do a little research, you'll find a plethora of advice on how to interpret the Bible. What follows is a summary of my own approach. I offer it in hopes of jumpstarting your thinking as you seek to construct your own methodology.

*Read the text, preferably in several translations.* Why read more than one translation? Doing so exposes us to the variety of ways in which different teams of translators have translated Hebrew and Greek terms, clauses, and sentences. While modern translations share much in common, the occasional differences in translation often reveal interpretative options you may want to pursue. My two favorite modern translations are the New American Standard Bible and the New Revised Standard Version.

*Jot down your initial reactions to the text.* Don't be afraid to note your gut-level response to a text. What insight does it offer about God, God's people, the world, or you? How do you feel about the text? Does it push you to feel encouraged, discouraged, hopeful, happy, angry, or frightened? Why? Later you can test the validity of your first response to the text, but resist the urge to self-edit at this stage in your study. Sometimes our initial reaction to a text proves insightful and useful, both to us and to others.

*Read two good commentaries in order to get other interpreters' takes on the literary and historical context of the text.* Most of us need help in order to start to imagine the culture in which a given biblical author lived and wrote. Fortunately, we live in an era when good, readable commentaries are readily available. Two of my favorite commentary sets are the Smyth & Helwys Bible Commentary series, and The New Interpreter's Bible series.

*Ask and answer a question: What might the text have meant to those who first heard the words or to the one who wrote the words?* Once you've done your homework with the text and the commentaries, engage your imagination. Try to get inside the hearts and minds of our ancient spiritual forebears. For example, for years I read Jesus' injunction to turn the other cheek as a call to refuse to respond to violence with violence. Only in recent years did I learn that Roman soldiers habitually backhanded conquered people, slaves, and even animals. The action showed that the soldier did not recognize the humanity of the person being slapped. Jesus told his followers to expose the other cheek to the soldier, which would require the soldier to use an open hand to slap. The open-handed slap, while still an insult, was delivered by one human to another. In essence, Jesus called his followers to practice peaceful resistance in a way that would confront their oppressors with their humanity. This single piece of historically grounded information enriched my understanding of passive resistance.

*Ask and answer a question: How do the words, deeds, and attitude of Jesus interact with the text?* Christians start with Jesus and work back into the Old Testament and out into the remainder of the New Testament. All biblical texts are evaluated in light of Jesus. For example, when you read Old Testament texts that call upon God's community to stone men, women, or even children for a variety of offenses, try reading John 8:1-11 at the same time, paying special attention to the statement of Jesus: *Let anyone among you who is without sin be the first to throw a stone at her.* Doing so may make us or the people we serve uncomfortable, but it honors our commitment to Christ as Lord.

*Try to write one to five sentences in which you articulate what you think is the meaning of the text.* You may find the exercise difficult at first, but the more you practice reducing your thoughts on a biblical text to a short, summary paragraph, the easier it becomes. Consider the following example based on Matthew 15:34: *Jesus can change the world (personal, church, local community, etc.) when we put all we actually have in his hands. As it turns out, what we actually have is enough for what needs doing in a given moment.* If you practice such a discipline on a regular basis, you gradually build quite a collection of personal commentary on the Bible. Read back through it occasionally. You will find that your collection becomes a valuable resource for your growth in Christ and your work with others.

*Ask and answer a question: If I applied the text in accordance with what I've come to believe it means, what about my life would be affirmed or changed?* Remember, it's okay to be affirmed by a biblical text. Some of us look only for how Scripture might challenge our beliefs. We need to be open to the comfort and affirmation the Scriptures sometimes provide. That being said, don't be afraid to allow a text to challenge even your core convictions and well-established habits of thought or deed. Deacons lead best when they submit to the affirming and convicting words of the Scriptures well interpreted.

*Maintain an attitude of prayer and humility as you seek to interpret and apply the text.* Pray as you read, study, reflect on, and apply a biblical text. Prayer opens us to the presence and work of Holy Spirit, who always stands ready to lead us toward wisdom. Work hard to cultivate humility. None of us grasps the full meaning and implications of the Scriptures. All our conclusions are tentative and subject to revision in light of additional knowledge and experience. As my wise, Presbyterian grandmother used to say, "You may be right, you may be wrong, or you may fall somewhere between truth and error. Live accordingly!"

*Test your conclusions through conversation with other serious students of the text.* Our working interpretations of Scripture are best tested in the context of a faith community. A deacon body ideally should be or become such a community, a safe and stimulating group of people with whom to explore the Scriptures. Who knows—if a deacon body functions as such a community, the church just might follow suit!

# Individual Exercises

1. Can you identify and describe in your own words the meta-narrative you bring to your study of the Scriptures?

2. Do you think your church family has one or more meta-narratives? Write one or two paragraphs describing the meta-narrative(s) you think exist within your church family.

3. How do you understand the divine inspiration of Scripture?

4. How does this brief overview of the history of the canon's development strike you?

5. How do you feel about the role the church played in testing and selecting the Scriptures that became the New Testament?

6. Using the suggestions in "Interpreting Scripture," offer your interpretations of Matthew 5:13-16.

7. Using the suggestions in "Interpreting Scripture," offer your interpretations of 1 Corinthians 8:1-13.

# Group Conversation

1. Share and discuss with the group the "meta-narratives" that each deacon brings to the study of Scripture.

2. Share and discuss with the group your understandings of the divine inspiration of Scripture.

3. Share and discuss with the group the history of the biblical canon's development.

4. Share and discuss with the group your different interpretations of Matthew 5:13-16 and 1 Corinthians 8:1-13.

# Deacons Learn Church History

The Church and each local congregation exist within the context of history. Is it possible for deacons to know and make good use of the nearly twenty centuries of church history?

Yes! Even as I write the term "yes," though, I can almost envision you closing the book and saying, "That's not for me." I understand. Church history is long, and the idea of diving into it is daunting. In addition, many (perhaps most) of us learned to dislike history in high school as we tried to memorize long lists of dates and names in order to pass a test.

Relax. I'll come at church history in a different way. In the space and time we have, I want to introduce you to some key developments and themes in the history of the church. We'll touch on just enough detail to demonstrate how church history affects congregations today.

Let's take a look at eight "snapshots" from church history.

## Snapshot 1: The First Century (mid-30s–100 CE)

My home church tended to believe the church began with unity in theology and practice, only to divide later in history. The truth is that the church began with a blend of unity and diversity. First- and second-generation Christians found unity in two confessions: "He is risen" and "Jesus is Lord." On the other hand, they often disagreed how best to interpret and apply such confessions.

Church governance structures also varied. Elders, such as James the brother of Jesus, seem to have led the Jerusalem church. As the church took root in other cities, some were governed by a combination of pastors and/or elders and deacons. The Corinthian church appears to have relied on a patronage system. Leading families opened their homes to the church, various groups in the church tended to cleave to a given patron, and the patrons exercised enormous influence. Much to the chagrin of folks from my particular heritage (Baptist), governance by congregational business meetings does not make an appearance in the first-century records, biblical or otherwise.

Worship may have been the greatest unifying factor. Most first-century churches probably practiced some variation on synagogue worship. Their services would have included prayer, readings from the Old Testament (and as the century advanced, perhaps readings from the four Gospels or some of Paul's letters), exposition, an offering (most often food to be shared with the hungry), and the Lord's Supper. A commitment to the instruction of those who wished to become Christ followers also constituted a unifying factor. No doubt custom varied from congregation to congregation, but such instruction probably included how to interpret the Old Testament in light of Jesus, what baptism signified, the core teachings of Jesus, and the congregation's expectations of converts.

The first century's greatest controversy centered on one question: *Does a Gentile have to become a Jew and observe Jewish law in order to become a Christian?* As Peter, Paul, and others took the gospel into the Gentile world, and as Gentile Christians grew more and more numerous, the question became acute. Acts 15 tells the story of the Jerusalem Conference in which Paul and Barnabas, the apostles, and the elders of the Jerusalem church attempted to find a compromise. As James the brother of Jesus put it,

> Therefore I have reached the decision we should not trouble those Gentiles who are turning to God, but we should write to them to abstain only from things polluted by idols and from fornication and from whatever has been strangled and from blood. For in every city, for generations past, Moses has had those who proclaim him, for he has been read aloud every Sabbath in the synagogues. (Acts 15:19-21)

James essentially called upon Gentile Christians to avoid practices that would offend Christians of Jewish origin.

Between the destruction of the temple in 70 CE and the end of the first century, the compromise collapsed. The synagogue and the church drew apart, so that by the end of the century the majority of Christians were Gentiles.

What might we take away from our snapshot of the first century? First, the church began as a sect within first-century Judaism and might have remained so had it not taken the gospel to the Gentiles. When Peter, Paul, and others baptized Gentiles without requiring them first to become Jews, the church was forced to wrestle with the limits of inclusion. By the end of the century, the church had moved beyond earlier assumptions and become fully open to all Gentiles. This would not be the last time the church faced the matter of who could be welcomed into the fellowship without special restrictions. The church found a way to move forward, engage many cultures with which it was in touch, and bring a diverse set of people to embrace Jesus as Lord and the church as their home. Just when it appeared the church might founder, it chose—however imperfectly—to expand its range of hospitality and so reach the first-century world for Christ.

# Snapshot 2: Constantine

Emperor Constantine the First (died 337 CE) ended the empire's persecution of Christianity. By the end of his life, he had effectively united the church and the Roman Empire. With a few exceptions, the functional union of church and state remained unchallenged until late in the Protestant Reformation.

Constantine spent most of his life trying to bring unity to his empire. Starting around 312 CE, he extended toleration to Christianity and all other religions. By 324 CE, he began to favor the church with active state support. From 330 CE until his death, he championed the church and persecuted other religions. Historians debate Constantine's motivations. Did he settle on the church primarily because he saw in it a way to unify a diverse and divided empire, or was he genuinely drawn to Christ? I think both motivations were in play. Still, Roman emperors had long used religion to help unify the empire, and I have no doubt Constantine followed such a policy.

The church soon learned that Constantine meant to have a say in theology and policy. He convened and participated in the Council of Nicea (325 CE), where he insisted the gathered bishops find common ground on a number of issues, especially the matter of the relationship of the Son to the Father. The council developed the Nicene Creed, which among other things taught the full equality of the Father and the Son. Bishops who refused to agree to the creed faced exile. For the first time in church history, the power of the state was brought to bear to enforce uniformity of belief within the church.

Constantine's patronage channeled state resources to the church to build and endow churches, support clergy, and finance the general work of the church. As we might expect, many citizens followed the emperor's lead, for Christianity now joined the list of social requirements for a successful career in government, the military, or business. Conquered tribes and client kings also accepted baptism. By the time of Constantine's death, a majority of the inhabitants and clients of the Roman Empire were nominally Christian. Left unanswered was the question of whether such civil religion meshed well with Christianity's historic emphasis on a new kind of life in Christ.

The challenge of the relationship between church and state runs throughout church history and remains a vexing issue in our day. Most modern historians suggest that the church always loses when it becomes a state-supported religion. Why do historians render such a verdict? First, the merger of the state with a particular religion leads to persecution of other religions. In addition, the union of church and state often results in persecution of minorities within the state-sponsored religion. When you read about the persecution of early Baptists or Quakers, Roger Williams, Protestants in some parts of the former Soviet Union, and others, remember that the roots of such situations run deep, harkening back to the first union of church and state under Constantine. Second, when citizenship and church membership essentially are one and the same, does the church lose something vital? How well do conviction, repentance, conversion, and a Jesus-centered counter-culturalism play out in the context of a church/state union? Can it do so?

Are you starting to see how history affects today's church, including your congregation? Let's move on to another snapshot.

# Snapshot 3: St. Francis

Most of us have heard the great prayer attributed to St. Francis (*Lord, make me an instrument of thy peace*, etc.). I think of Francis as the exemplar of what the monastic tradition contributes to Christianity. The monastic movement began in the second century CE. Under the leadership of Gregory the Great, who became Pope around 590 CE, monasticism became the means by which Christianity in the West was preserved during the so-called "Dark Ages."

Monasteries and convents preserved many of the writings and insights of the church fathers and mothers, not to mention much of the literature of ancient Rome and Greece. Such resources later paved the way for the rejuvenation of western civilization.

Just as important, the monastic movement stood as a living, though imperfect, reminder of Jesus' call to leave all and follow him. At its best, monasticism encouraged people caught up in culture and cultural religion to envision and embrace a Christ-centered, counter-cultural way of life.

Francis was born in 1182 CE to a well-to-do family in Assisi, Italy. As a boy and young man, he showed little inclination to responsibility or religion. The experience of being a prisoner of war for a time, followed by a serious illness, seems to have prompted his religious conversion. In 1208, Francis embraced a life mission: he would imitate Christ, embrace poverty, and obey Christ's commands as fully as possible. Soon, followers began to join him. Francis wrote guidelines for them to follow, mostly drawn from the commands of Jesus. He sent them out two by two to preach repentance, care for the sick and outcasts, and practice poverty.

Francis himself became best known for his devotion to prayer, his love of the natural world coupled with an ability to see God in nature, and his increasing sense of identification with Christ. He saw the image of God in all others and nature, and the unity of all things in God. Today, Francis remains a beloved figure among Roman Catholics and Protestants.

Francis's life exemplifies core themes from monasticism that remain in play today: following Jesus as the heart of the Christian life, compassion and care for the least of these, and embracing the creation as worthy of love and revelatory of God. What difference might it make in your congregation if members learned to desire to follow the commands of Jesus more than anything else? Is it still possible for Christians to hear the call of Jesus to leave all and follow him? Can we imagine the life of a Christian or congregation in which the creation is valued and loved for its own sake rather than the profit we might squeeze from it? Is it really possible for Christians or congregations to devote themselves to preaching the good news and caring for the sick, outcast, and marginalized? The life of Francis tells us all such things are possible.

# Snapshot 4: The Reformation

Martin Luther, a monk and priest and scholar, supposedly nailed 95 Theses to the door of the church in Wittenberg, Germany, on October 31, 1517, and the Protestant Reformation began. Actually, reformers had been at work within Roman Catholicism for generations before Luther. He and those who came after him (Calvin, Zwingli, and others) arrived on the scene as several cultural factors attained enough momentum to make drastic changes possible. Rising nationalism conditioned rulers and their subjects to consider distancing themselves from foreign authorities, including Rome. The Renaissance with its recovery of knowledge of Greek and Hebrew (the languages in which the New Testament and Old Testament were written) and the writings of Rome and Greece fueled a growing desire to investigate the ancient sources of religion and culture. Abuses on the part of the established church (the most famous being indulgences) fed the hunger for reform as well.

Luther did not set out to establish another branch of Christianity. Instead, he wanted to reform or purify the Roman Catholicism of his day. Ironically, many of the abuses he wished to correct were dealt with later by the Roman Catholic Church, as it underwent its own reformation.

In the decades and centuries after Luther, Protestants demonstrated a flair for divisions. They divided into several large groups: Lutherans, Reform (Calvinists), Anglican, and Radical. The trend continues to this day. My own branch of the faith (Baptist) features forty or more separate denominations in the United States alone.

Protestantism's core themes continue to interface with the life of the church. These include a desire to base the Christian life and the life of the church on the Scriptures, a tendency to take on the characteristics of the culture in which it exists, a commitment to spread its version of the gospel, and tension between individual religious freedom and religious authority figures or institutions.

The core strength of the Protestant tradition is that it pushes us to engage the Scriptures. At its best, the tradition produces people who take seriously the teachings of Jesus, interpret the rest of Scripture in light of Jesus, and shape their lives to conform to the image of Jesus. At its worst, the tradition encourages self-righteousness, division, and the creation of ever smaller circles of fellowship.

Deacons best serve a congregation when they model how to maximize the strengths of Protestantism while minimizing the impact of its weaknesses.

# Snapshot 5: Revivalism

In August 1801 in Cane Ridge, Kentucky, revival broke out during a camp meeting. Barton Stone, a Presbyterian minister, convened the event. A crowd of between ten and twenty-five thousand people gathered. Multiple preachers proclaimed the gospel from atop crude platforms or tree trunks. At some point, people began to respond. Untold numbers of people either became Christians or renewed their faith during the meeting.

The Cane Ridge meeting, and the thousands of camp and revival meetings that followed it, remodeled American church life. Revival meetings became the normative way, at least in the "West" of the nineteenth century, to expand the reach of Christianity and establish new churches. The Methodists, Baptists, and Presbyterians of the region embraced the new approach and enjoyed enormous numerical growth.

Several elements of the movement took root in many denominations and continue to affect outlook and practice to this day.

Fervent preaching and an invitation to repent, give one's life to Christ, and join a church became a standard feature of church life. At the camp meetings, such calls often came at the end of a sermon. People were invited to come to the front of the gathering and take a place on a "mourner's bench" (often a log). There, pastors and others would pray with them, assist them as they worked through their emotions, and encourage them to give their lives to Christ. Until this point in time, most churches in America encouraged prospective Christians to talk with the pastor, reflect carefully on what it meant to follow Jesus, and take their time in making a decision. The camp meetings changed all that for many churches and denominations. Now sermons and worship services were expected to focus on evangelism, conclude with a call to repentance, and be measured by whether someone "walked the aisle." By the end of the nineteenth century, many Christians assumed that this had always been the pattern of Christian worship and evangelism.

Revivalism led to the development of "methods" for leading people to make decisions for Christ. At the risk of oversimplification, the following elements eventually took hold: A professional evangelist was engaged to hold a revival meeting. Large numbers of individual churches and individuals in a city or region were enlisted to pray for and financially support the approaching revival. Churches and individuals were encouraged to identify, invite, and bring friends and acquaintances to the event. The revival meeting itself was preceded by days or weeks of home prayer meetings. Worship services featured strong congregational singing, testimonies, sermons designed to expose individual sin and the need for repentance, "drawing the net" (using sales techniques to identify and demolish objections to making a decision), a public invitation and a mourner's bench or the equivalent, counseling on the spot, and subsequent follow-up by churches. In the process, thousands of people made professions of faith and became church members.

As time went on, the search for personal salvation tended to morph from a journey into a decision made in an instant.

Some churches and denominations, of course, resisted such developments, preferring a more traditional approach to worship and disciple-making. In either case, though, churches and denominations hardened with regard to the matter and usually questioned the validity of the opposite approach.

Consider your congregation. Does revivalism continue to affect the life of the congregation, even if the members have never heard of it? Can you identify some disagreements within the congregation, either among members or between the congregation and clergy, that are rooted in the legacy of revivalism? Do you think a working knowledge of the continuing influence of revivalism might help the church better navigate such times?

# Snapshot 6: Global Religion

In the aftermath of the Reformation, both Protestants and Roman Catholics ramped up their mission endeavors, not only because of competition with one another but also because of their shared determination to extend the reach of the gospel. Christianity spread throughout all the continents. Regions, over time, developed indigenous forms of Christianity. Even as I write these words, the fastest-growing Christian bodies in the world are found in Asia, Africa, and South America. Most projections suggest that the center of Christianity will shift to these regions over the next few decades. Christianity is a global religion.

And Christianity is not alone. As late as the mid-twentieth century, most of us knew of other major religions or ways of life such as Islam, Hinduism, Buddhism, Judaism, and the like. Outside of a handful of major cities, though, we seldom encountered and grew to know people from such traditions.

Now the world's major religions rub shoulders via communications media, business, education, and politics. Adherents live, shop, school, and recreate alongside one another in the United States and other nations. The world has come to us, and we have gone into the world.

There's nothing abstract about the matter. My son grew up going to school with people from multiple branches of Christianity and other world religions. His friends came from Christian, Muslim, Hindu, Jewish, and Buddhist contexts, plus a smattering of other religious communities. He has never known a world with religious, racial, or intellectual borders. The 9/11 terrorist attack occurred during his high school years. He joined friends from the various religious communities in Memphis, Tennessee, to foster improved communications, acceptance, and nonviolence in the city.

We are living through a hinge period in history, a time when Christians of various kinds are talking among themselves, holding conversations (some civil, some heated) about how best to engage global Christianity and world religions. Conversations are also going on between Christianity and other world religions. Such conversations affect (and will affect) the church's self-perception, doctrine, and practice.

For example, Christians from various branches of Christianity even now are wrestling with three options with regard to salvation: exclusivism, inclusivism, or pluralism. Exclusivists maintain that salvation is available only to those who hear and receive the gospel as preached by the church. Those who adopt an inclusive approach usually say that people of other religions might still be saved by God's grace, if their lives are devoted to the ideals of Christ, whether or not they know of Christ. Pluralists tend to argue that all religions may guide a person into salvation. All three perspectives are found in many congregations.

What might deacons do to help congregations grapple with a world in which global Christianity and global religions must find ways to live together? My suggestion is to start small. Devote at least one meeting per year and a portion of an annual deacon retreat to exploring the content and practice of various forms of Christianity and other world religions. Use the opportunity to learn about and analyze stories of congregations who have dealt well (in whatever manner) with the challenge and opportunity of living in an increasingly global culture.

# Snapshot 7: The Baptist Tradition

In 1609 in Amsterdam, John Smyth, an Anglican turned Separatist Puritan, embraced believer's baptism as the basis for gathering a church. He baptized himself by pouring water over his head, did the same for a layman named Thomas Helwys, and led their followers to follow suit. Smyth soon moved on to become a Mennonite. Helwys, though, led the group back to England, where he founded a church at Spitalfield, a section of London.

Helwys, far more than Smyth, set the tone of the early Baptist movement. He argued for believer's baptism (though he did not require immersion), free will, religious liberty, and separation of church and state. Church officers, he wrote, should be selected by the local congregation, and both men and women could serve as deacons. His type of Baptists soon became known as General Baptists. By the time he died (1624), at least five General Baptist churches existed. Their number increased to forty-seven by 1650.

Another kind of Baptist emerged in 1638 from a Separatist Puritan congregation in London. These Baptists accepted much of John Calvin's theology. They articulated their beliefs in 1644 in a document called "The London Confession." Their beliefs included limited atonement, perseverance of the saints, predestination of the elect and non-elect, believer's baptism, the Scriptures as the supreme authority in the life of the church, religious freedom, and the church's responsibility to select its officers.

Roger Williams founded the first Baptist church in America at Providence, Rhode Island, in 1639. His primary contribution to Baptist life lay in his insistence on complete religious liberty (including the right to reject religion) and separation of church and state. Baptists remained a minority movement in America, even as they spread into most of the colonies. Two major traditions emerged: the Regular Baptists and the Separate Baptists. Regular Baptists, represented by the First Baptist Church of Charleston, valued order in worship, an educated clergy, Calvinism, confessions of faith, and restrictions on the role of women. Separate Baptists, represented by Sandy Creek Baptist Church, favored a modified Calvinism that left room for human free will, evangelism, and fervent worship and preaching. They distrusted confessions of faith and an educated clergy, and they made room for women to serve as church officers and preach. In 1845, the two traditions merged uneasily in the newly formed Southern Baptist Convention.

By the mid-twentieth century, Baptists were the second largest group of Christians in the United States and were represented in numerous other countries. With over forty denominations in the United States, Baptists varied considerably in the practice of church life with regard to worship styles, theological emphases, the role of men and women, baptism, the Lord's Supper, and social engagement. Most efforts to develop and enforce theological unity among Baptists simply led to divisions and the formation of new Baptist bodies.

That being said, most Baptist bodies accepted several core convictions: priesthood of the believer, religious freedom, church freedom, and separation of church and state. Priesthood of the believer meant individuals stood free and responsible for themselves before God. With regard to church freedom, most Baptists believed congregations to be autonomous: free and responsible to order their beliefs and practice. Religious liberty and separation of church and state went together. Baptists generally believed all people should be free to determine their own response to God and religion (even to reject God and religion) without interference or support from the state. The separation of church and state (often summarized as "a free church in a free church") secured such freedom.

Deacons best serve their congregations when they become acquainted with the broad outline of Baptist history and help their congregations do the same.

# Individual Exercises

1. Select one of the "snapshots" from church history and ask what issues, characteristics, practices, or challenges in your church are informed by them.

2. What other "snapshots" of church history might you like to explore and why?

3. Does it make a difference when we recognize a situation's historical roots versus seeing it in terms of right or wrong? If so, explain.

# Group Conversation

1. Have each deacon share one thing from the historical snapshots that he or she thinks would be good for your church to adopt (for example, Franciscan or monastic prayer practices), and discuss how this might be implemented in your congregation.

2. Having read the snapshots, have the deacons name ways of doing church that they have inherited from other eras of church history. Have them discuss which ones are important to strengthen in their congregation's life; ones they may wish to deemphasize; or ones they might choose to introduce anew (for example, Lord's Supper practices; nature of ordination; types of prayer; church/state relationships).

3. Have the deacons discuss the Baptist snapshot, naming ways your congregation continues the early Baptist tradition and ways your congregation varies from it. Discuss whether these similarities and differences are helpful or harmful for contemporary Baptist congregational life.

4. Assign each deacon a snapshot, and have him or her try to convince the other deacons to change the congregation to fit that type of historical Christianity. What does this exercise teach you about the advantages and disadvantages of each perspective?

# Deacons Think Theologically

The root meaning of the term "theology" is "thinking about God" or "words about God." All Christians practice theology. We can't escape it. One of my friends likes to say that the moment someone in the New Testament era proclaimed the confession, "Jesus is Lord," another Christian responded, "Great. Now what does that mean?"

How might we think and talk about God? What are the possibilities and limits of language? When it comes to thinking about God, how many starting points exist? Where does thinking about God lead with reference to everything else? What can we know about God? These and other questions drive the theological task.

Modern Christian theology comes in numerous flavors or sub-disciplines of the general discipline of theology: systematic, pastoral, confessional, biblical, experiential, existential, philosophical, mystical, liberation, and denominational to name a few. Few of us, deacons included, become professional theologians, but it's useful to recognize that Christians come at the task from a variety of starting places. Perhaps God takes delight in meeting us where we are. If we're philosophically inclined, God most likely engages us through philosophy. On the other hand, if we learn best through experience, God meets us there, and so on.

A few years ago, a pastor shared the following story with several of us. One of his long-term members, a woman respected by the congregation, fell under the spell of a television preacher. She began to insist that Christians ought to expect God to give them whatever they dreamed they should have. Money, success in business, a new house, and good health topped her list. When some in the church challenged her, she responded that they lacked the right kind of faith. She sparked a low-intensity controversy in the church. Finally, she left the congregation.

Sound familiar? Nowadays, theologies—ways of thinking about God—knock on the church's door quite often. In fact, they walk through the door of the church via media preachers, blogs, emails, and books. Individual Christians and entire congregations sometimes experience considerable confusion and pain as a result.

Deacons need to know how to help a congregation evaluate theologies. While no method is foolproof, learning to ask the following questions of a theology might be helpful.

*Is it centered on Christ?* Does the theology bring to mind the Jesus we find in the four Gospels? Can you imagine Jesus endorsing its core elements? How does the Sermon on the Mount, the way Jesus dealt with people, Jesus' sacrifice of self, and Jesus' attitude toward God match up with the goals of the theology in question? Do the assumptions, methods, and aspirations of the theology correspond to any of the temptations Jesus rejected in the wilderness? If so, what might that imply about the theology? Remember, Jesus said that those who had seen him had seen the Father. When you examine a theology, ask if it reveals the God seen in Jesus.

*Does it model Christ-like love as the measure of the Christian life?* Jesus insisted his followers would become people who practice love toward even their enemies, pray for those who despitefully used them, and eschew the sword in favor of peace. In 1 Corinthians 13, Paul describes Christians as those who practice love, and he outlines the attributes of such love: "Love is patient; love is kind; love is not envious or boastful or arrogant or rude. It does not insist on its own way; it is not irritable or resentful; it does not rejoice in wrongdoing, but rejoices in the truth. It bears all things, believes all things, hopes all things, endures all things" (vv. 4-7). Jesus taught that two commandments summed up Christian theology and life: love God without holding back anything, and love your neighbor as yourself. The Lord also said others would know we were his disciples by our love for one another. Does the theology under review measure up to the test of Christ-like love?

*Does it bond us to the Christian community or encourage separation from the Christian community?* In John 17, Jesus prays for his disciples, and among other things, he asks God to ensure "that they may all be one. As you, Father, are in me and I am in you, may they also be in us. . . . The glory that you have given me I have given them, so that they may be one, as we are one." I've heard many people teach that Christians should pursue unity on the basis of theology and, if such unity cannot be forged or enforced, should separate from one another. Such people assume that unity grows from theological agreement. Jesus, though, starts at a difference place. He grounds our unity in his relationship with God, and he prays that nothing we may believe or do will be allowed to obscure our bond with one another. Does the theology under consideration accord well with Christ's prayer for the unity of his followers?

*Does it provide for sharing the gospel and ministering to others as if to Jesus?* Jesus shared the good news of God's sacrificial love. He preached, taught, and modeled such love. Following the resurrection, Jesus instructed his disciples to do the same. Jesus also told the parable of the sheep and goats, in which he commissioned Christians to minister to all others as though they were ministering to Christ. When a theology comes knocking on the door of your congregation, check to see if it provides for sharing and living out such a gospel.

*Does it expand or contract the circle of the church's fellowship?* Jesus told his disciples he had followers whom they did not know. Paul insisted that the gospel be preached without strings attached. Take a look at the pattern of the church's expansion in the New Testament. Again and again, the church finds it must enlarge its circle of fellowship if it is to fulfill the expectations of Jesus. More often than not, some within the church fear or oppose such expansion. The Holy Spirit, though, pushes the matter and brings it to pass with the help of those in the church who are willing to listen to the Spirit. Will the theology in question work well with the Holy Spirit's expansionist bent?

No doubt, you can think of other questions to ask. Remember, congregations usually need help to evaluate and respond to theologies that knock on the doors of the church. Deacons can develop, model, and teach solid ways to deal well with such theologies.

# My Approach to Theology

Take my own approach to theology as an example. I describe it as a blend of experiential, biblical, and mystical. Having served as a pastor for decades, I naturally draw on experience to fashion my take on God. When you walk alongside people in all life cycles, live with them through joy and grief, practice worship in their company, and converse with them about every conceivable matter—well, let's just say such a life inevitably feeds into one's theology.

We should not be surprised that *experience* plays a significant role in the theology of many of us. After all, Jesus often uses the experiences of life to talk about God. He speaks of God as loving parent, farmer, physician, a wind that blows where it will, and the like. Jesus draws on earthy images to illustrate what life with God is like: sowing seed, looking for lost coins, landlords and tenants, roadside encounters, and such.

I also draw on the *Scriptures*, again following the lead of Jesus. Jesus uses the Scriptures (the Old Testament) in a particular way. He focuses on what the Scriptures have to say about God's love for people, disdain for self-serving theologies, desire to build a human community grounded in self-giving love, and intent to redeem not only humanity but all of creation. He boils all the Law down to two matters: love God without reservation, and love others as you love yourself. Jesus consistently interprets and applies the Scriptures in light of the two commands. As I turn to the Scriptures to help shape my theology, I try to use the method of Jesus. It's amazing how much clutter is cleared away by such an approach.

Finally, I mentioned *mystical* theology. The term carries a number of meanings, but when I use it, I'm talking about an approach to theology that starts by acknowledging the limits of language. All language about God falls short of the reality of God; all language about God is analogical. I also mean that I do theology on the basis of a conviction: all people are made in the image of God. The work of the church is to seek and find that image in all of us, bring it to the surface, and help us learn to live into it.

I've shared a bit about my own approach to theology not to tell you what to think about God but to illustrate how one person (namely, me) does his thinking about God.

# Guidelines for Theological Thinking

While most of us are not professional theologians, we can learn and model healthy ways of doing theology. A little research will uncover numerous suggestions for how to do so. I offer the following guidelines for consideration. My colleagues and I have found them useful.

*Start with and stick with Jesus.* Yes, this is virtually the same point with which I began the previous list. Glad to see you're paying attention! Christians build theologies in response to the God they experience best in Jesus. I've always found it most helpful to start with the Sermon on the Mount, move to the commissions (make disciples, love God and neighbor and self, minister to all as if to Jesus), and throw in the parables of Jesus. As I do so, I keep Paul's admonition in mind: I seek to know the mindset of Christ and to nurture the same mindset for myself. If you're going to construct a Christian theology, start with and stick with Jesus.

*Acknowledge and remember the contingency of all theological language.* God cannot be described or captured by human language. Perhaps that is the reason God chose to reveal himself best through a particular human life, that of Jesus. Nonetheless, we must use words to describe God as best we may. Trouble is, we fall in love with our own words. Many times I've been caught in a conversation with a fellow Christian who insists that I cannot be right with God until I use the same terms as he or she to describe God. Read back through the Scriptures, and you'll find quite a number of words and phrases that attempt to describe God: king, shepherd, father, mother, a bird sheltering chicks beneath its wings, spirit, fire, cloud—the list becomes quite long. God transcends our words. Use words, but do not become so attached to them that you are unable to turn loose of them, appreciate another's chosen words, or move on to embrace new words.

*Never be afraid to affirm, discard, or modify a theological concept in the name of Jesus.* In the first church I served, one of my friends was devoted to Jesus yet also a racist. She had fled the city to avoid having to interact daily with people of other races. When I asked her about the matter, she assured me the Bible taught that black people were inferior and that the races were to be segregated. Years later, I returned to that congregation to serve as its interim pastor. My friend was still there. By then she was known as a local advocate for the poor, including black people. She brought children of all colors to Vacation Bible School and Sunday school. I asked her what had happened. She answered, "Jesus changed my mind." My friend had a living theology, one that allowed her to change her mind as she came to know Jesus better.

*Go where your developing theology takes you, live with the results, and see how they wear.* As you develop your theology, try it out in daily life. Test it as you read the Scriptures, pray, and minister to others. What are the results? Is the theology pushing and pulling you toward Christ-likeness in all settings? If not, why not? What is working and what might need reevaluation?

*Do not go it alone.* Long ago, I had a friend who might best be described as a theological loner. He insisted on doing his theological work alone. When he completed a portion of his theology, he would share it with us and then step back, expecting us to say, "That's amazing. Why didn't we think of that? Your insight changes everything." The truth of the matter is that his theological constructs usually mirrored his personal eccentricities and prejudices. When exposed to outside scrutiny, his frameworks fell apart. Good theologies develop best in the context of conversation with trusted friends, both those who tend to agree with us and those who might disagree with us. Build your theology in the midst of such a community.

*Do not play to win.* I can't speak for other cultures, but most Americans I know love to compete. Our motto is captured in a saying: "If you don't play to win, you play to lose." Strangely enough, Christians who follow the one who "lost" his life on a cross often buy in to such a philosophy. When it comes to theology, the general history of the church and congregational histories are littered with wreckage from this "winner take all" approach. Do you remember what I wrote about Jesus' take on Christian unity? Jesus grounds our unity in his unity with God. Within that unity, we can think, talk, and debate theologies in order to help one another in our walk with Christ. My hunch is that the diversity of our viewpoints improves the chances of our helping one another see more of the fullness of God. When we succumb to the temptation to try to win an argument, we sin against the unity of Christ's Body, violate the purpose of theological inquiry, and diminish our opportunity to learn more about God.

*Never take yourself too seriously!* When I first began to serve as the pastor of a church, an older minister took me under his wing. To my untutored eye, he seemed to be a person who had done everything I could ever dream of doing. Nearly everyone I knew regarded him as a nearly perfect combination of scholar, pastor, journalist, editor, and denominational statesman. One day over lunch, I worked up enough courage to ask him the secret of his successful life. "My friend," he said, "devotion to God, good friends, lots of serious study, hard work, and a certain flexibility have served me well. Looking back, though, I think the real secret is this: I learned never to take myself too seriously." With regard to doing theology, the trick is never to bind our sense of worth to our theology. Our worth is found in and guaranteed by God. Think instead of theology as a kind of holy play through which we refresh ourselves and delight God.

*Do theology as an act of worship.* As you construct, test, refine, and live into your theology, remember to do so within the larger framework of worship. After all, the highest purpose of our lives, whether individually or as the church, is the worship of God. I sometimes think we might build and use theologies more wisely if we always started and ended such work with prayer.

To that end, here's my final suggestion. *Use two prayers to frame the times in which you work individually or with others at the theological task.* I've found that two prayers, one from the Bible and the other from church history, help keep me on track.

Open your work by reciting the Lord's Prayer. Use whichever translation you like. In this case, I prefer the King James Version.

Our Father which art in heaven, hallowed be thy name. Thy kingdom come. Thy will be done in earth, as it is in heaven. Give us this day our daily bread. And forgive us our debts, as we forgive our debtors. And lead us not into temptation, but deliver us from evil: For thine is the kingdom, and the power, and the glory, for ever. Amen. (Matt 6:9-13)

This prayer sets the tone and goal of all Christian theological endeavors. Whatever we come to think and say about God should mirror the goals embedded in the Lord's Prayer.

I also find it useful to conclude a period of theological work by saying a prayer attributed to St. Francis. This prayer is found in several forms. I find the following one most useful.

Lord, make me an instrument of thy peace. Where there is hatred, let me sow love; where there is injury, pardon; where there is doubt, faith; where there is despair, hope; where there is darkness, light; where there is sadness, joy.

O Divine Master, grant that I may not so much seek to be consoled as to console; to be understood, as to understand; to be loved, as to love; for it is in giving that we receive, it is in pardoning that we are pardoned, and it is in dying that we are born to eternal life.

The prayer of Francis reminds us that the goal of all good Christian theology is the formation and living of a Christ-like life, both as individuals and as congregations.

When we frame our theological work within the two prayers, we remember that all theologies fall within the larger framework of worship.

Perhaps deacons, being a small body within the larger body of a congregation, can practice doing theology as a worshiping community. The more deacons do so, the more likely their congregations will, too.

# Individual Exercises

1. Name one to three theologies that have come knocking on the doors of your church. How did your church deal (or not deal) with each? Select one of the theologies and test it by applying the questions suggested by the author (you may have to do some reading or online research). What conclusions did you reach about the theology?

2. Try thinking theologically by doing the follow exercise. Start with the common theological dictum, "God is sovereign." Now play with the dictum by applying the nine guidelines suggested by the author. As you work through the guidelines, how does the meaning of "God is sovereign" change in content or tone?

3. How can we recognize the dynamic nature of Christian theology while attempting to practice it?

4. How can deacons and church leaders manage the differences between daily living in the world and their commitment to Christian theology?

5. How can we create a community of theological reflection and development within our congregation?

# Group Conversation

1. How might we begin our conversation about individual theology among our deacon body? (Perhaps we could start by clarifying our theology about Jesus.)

2. What steps could we take to help our lay leadership develop their theology?

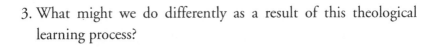

3. What might we do differently as a result of this theological learning process?

4. Break into small groups. Discuss and outline the mindset of Christ. Do not attempt to reach consensus. Instead, simply list the characteristics identified by each group member. Share the results with the larger group.

5. Identify and discuss one theological concept you might be willing to adopt or discard in light of the conversation about the mindset of Christ.

6. Discuss the following question: "If we were to adopt or discard a given theological concept in light of the mindset of Christ, how might we process the action with the congregation, and what about our congregation would need to change?"

# What Do Deacons Need to Do?

The third question has to do with conduct and the behavioral side of Christian discipleship. Our actions in everyday life, and sometimes our non-actions, reveal our priorities, values, and commitments. What we actually do in the particular circumstances of our lives says a lot about our faith. Scripture refers to our actions as "deeds" or "works."

**Session 7: Deacons Practice Public Worship and Private Prayer**

This session inspires conversation about public worship and private prayer. Prayer and worship are two of the most essential actions for Christians, and deacons should be faithful practitioners and congregational leaders in both. The individual exercises and group questions are intended to instruct, inspire, and challenge us in what can only be called a mystery.

**Session 8: Deacons Practice Partnership in God's Mission**

This session inspires conversation about participating in God's reconciling mission to the world by "making disciples" of others. Christ calls each of us to follow him, become like him, and be his presence to others in both word and deed. The individual exercises and group questions invite us to examine how faithful we are in witness and ministry, both as individuals and as congregations.

## Session 9: Deacons Practice Creative and Generous Stewardship

This session inspires conversation about the practice of Christian stewardship. How we use our time, money, energy, and influence is a significant measurement of Christian discipleship. Particular emphasis is given to the stewardship of financial resources and material possessions. Both the individual exercises and group study on three biblical texts focus on contentment and generosity, challenging deacons to set an example in stewardship.

# Deacons Practice Public Worship and Private Prayer

In the next sessions, we focus on what deacons *do* because of who they *are* as God's beloved children and as partners in God's mission in the world, and because of what they *know* (and continue to learn) about the will and way of Jesus revealed through Scripture, church history, and theology. We'll pay particular attention to these practices: (1) public and shared worship; (2) private and personal prayer; (3) creative and generous stewardship of our entire lives; and (4) partnership in God's mission to heal creation and reconcile humanity.

We learn faithful Christian living and effective Christian leading by means of *practice*. The classical professions are often called "practices," and preparing for them includes early work under the tutelage of people who have experience and wisdom to share. Doctors do internships and residencies; educators engage in practice teaching; lawyers serve as clerks; and counselors offer therapy under close supervision.

It's the same with plumbers, electricians, carpenters, and mechanics; they apprentice themselves to more advanced and skilled "masters" who provide them on-the-job training.

It's also true with many artists and most athletes: they yoke themselves to gifted teachers, mentors, or coaches who nurture and shape their abilities.

Like most people who like to cook, I have a shelf full of cookbooks, but I didn't learn to cook by reading. I learned to cook by cooking. Early on, I watched others, especially my mother and grandmothers, and over time they let me help them. Eventually, as I did what I saw them do, I could cook simple meals on my own: spaghetti sauce and pasta; fried chicken, mashed potatoes, and half-runner green beans; from-scratch pancakes and scrambled eggs with cheese.

Then, when Anita and I were in seminary, I worked as a waiter at *Kienle's*, a small German restaurant on the east side of Louisville. Adi and Marlene, the owners, operated an upscale deli by day and a formal restaurant at night. Adi was the chef. The business was too small for him to afford apprentices, so he allowed me to work alongside him, chopping vegetables, preparing stocks and sauces, and making salads. It was rigorous on-the-job training in kitchen basics.

So I learned to cook by cooking in the company of people who were more experienced than I was, who included me in what they were doing, and who taught me by letting me practice alongside them. When I cook dinner for my family, as I do several nights a week, I am still practicing, still learning-by-doing and doing what I have learned.

Some of our best learning—and living—comes as a result of *practicing*, especially practicing in community, in mutually encouraging relationship with others. For that reason, deacons become more effective Christian leaders—and more faithful followers of Jesus—when they learn by doing, hone their skills by repetition, and enhance their effectiveness by training. Regular practice, often alongside others, prepares deacons to become better servant leaders.

There are times when we don't *feel* like doing what the teachings and example of Jesus call for us to do. Our emotions don't align with his expectations; our hearts aren't in it. It can feel awkward and even insincere to act in ways that are out of sync with how we feel.

Philosopher of pragmatism and pioneering psychologist William James articulated a helpful insight: "Action seems to follow feeling, but really action and feeling go together; and by regulating the action, which is under the more direct control of the will, we can indirectly regulate the feeling, which is not."[6] In other words, it's not always possible to feel our way into a new way of acting; sometimes we have to act our way into a new way of feeling.

If we wait on our feelings to guide us to live in some of the ways Jesus intends—praying for enemies, giving away our hard-earned money, or forgiving people who have wronged us—we might not ever do those kinds of things. We have to act first and let our feeling catch up.

To some people, acting our way into a new way of feeling sounds hypocritical, like pious pretending. It's not hypocrisy, though, if the motive for doing what we don't yet feel like doing is to become more faithful and more like Jesus than we are. It's only hypocrisy if our motives are to impress other people—to gain the reward of reputation without doing the work of character building.

# The Practice of Public Worship

Gathering with other followers of Jesus for shared and public worship of God and engaging in a pattern of frequent personal and private prayer are central practices for all Christians and, certainly, for deacons. We will consider the practice of prayer in the next section of this chapter. Here, we affirm that shared worship is a way for deacons to nurture their connection with God and others, to bear witness to the greatness and grace of God, and to lead others, by example, to a recognition of the indispensable importance of worship in a life of faith.

Too often, when worship is a topic of conversation in a church, discussion quickly focuses on structure and style. We use terms like "formal," "informal," "liturgical," "contemporary," and "emerging." We debate the value of pipe organs, pianos, and orchestras in tension with synthesizers, drums, and praise bands. Choices between hymnals and projector screens and between "Sunday clothes" (or robes) and casual clothes for worship leaders become symbols of assumptions and philosophies about worship.

What sometimes gets lost in our worship conversations is that worship is "for God" more than "for us"; therefore, what matters most, whatever the structure and style of our gatherings, is the quality and genuineness of our offering ourselves to God in "wonder, love, and praise." The Apostle Paul wrote to his friends in Rome about offering our entire selves to God:

> I appeal to you therefore, brothers and sisters, by the mercies of God, to present your bodies as a living sacrifice, holy and acceptable to God, which is your spiritual worship. Do not be conformed to this world, but be transformed by the renewing of your minds, so that you may discern what is the will of God— what is good and acceptable and perfect. (Rom 12:1-2)

It might seem puzzling that Paul said, "Present your bodies to God," especially since we have a tendency to think of worship as a "spiritual" and "emotional" practice. For Paul, though, there was no other self than an embodied self: to offer our bodies to God is to offer our whole selves, the totality of our lives. As Eugene Peterson translated Paul's words, "Take your everyday, ordinary life—your sleeping, eating, going-to-work, and walking-around life—and place it before God as an offering" (Rom 12:1, *Message*).

One effect of worship is to "renew of our minds," which it does primarily by challenging the dominant values of our culture. Cornelius Plantinga, Jr., and Sue Rozeboom write,

> Suppose a son strays from home and adopts a drug-dealer as his parent-figure. The boy is with this dealer all the time, talking like him, walking like him, borrowing his Rolex, driving his Cadillac. The boy's mother watches with growing alarm. She has cleaned office buildings for years, just to satisfy her son's appetite and send him to a private school. She has made him do homework, take out the trash, and get enough sleep. She was determined to do all she could to insulate her son against the blandishments of easy money. She and her son have stood against the world. Now a stranger has gotten in between them.
>
> Might there be a time when, given her history of care and self-sacrifice, this mother would have to lay out her resume for her son? With quivering lip, this fine woman declares, "Son, don't neglect me. Don't forget that I'm your mother, and that there is no one else like me. There is no one like me on the street. I am the only one who really loves you and always will." . . . She's out to save her son, and she'll do whatever it takes.[7]

Our culture's assumptions, patterns, and expectations can be like strangers who get between us and God. These strangers don't know us and love us the way God knows and loves us. They can't see the beauty and wonder God sees in us. They lie to us about who we are and who God is.

Contrary to the pervasive insistence of our culture, we are not what we earn and own, busyness is not a sign of importance, self-worth doesn't depend on net worth, and vulnerability isn't weakness. "This world" tells us that we aren't talented enough, handsome enough, beautiful enough, strong enough, or smart enough to be loved. These are the lies of a stranger that conform us to lives of anxiety, fear, envy, and loneliness. Worship calls us back, again and again, to the God who loves us.

For their own life of faith—to offer themselves in grateful praise to God and to experience the renewal of their minds—deacons need to gather regularly with the community of faith for worship. It's a responsibility they carry as leaders—part of their witness and example. Deacons might also participate in worship leadership, sometimes by the simple but important tasks of greeting fellow worshipers, collecting offerings, or serving the Lord's Supper. Such tasks reflect the servanthood that is part of being a deacon, and they help model the ways Christians give themselves for the sake of others. Sometimes, deacons will read Scripture or offer prayers. Being thoughtfully prepared to do these things well demonstrates the importance of worship.

# The Practice of Personal Prayer

Most of us realize that, to live and lead in the ways of Jesus, we need resources higher and deeper than our own. That sense of need draws us to the practice of personal prayer, a practice that Jesus found necessary for nurturing his sense of identity and calling. The Gospel of Luke highlights the role prayer played in Jesus' life. More than the other Gospels, Luke presents Jesus as a person who moved to the rhythms of prayer.

Luke alone tells us that while Jesus was praying after his baptism, he saw the heavens opened, felt the Holy Spirit descend upon him, and heard a voice from heaven say to him, "You are my son, the Beloved; with you I am well pleased" (Luke 3:21-22). Luke describes Jesus' frequent retreats from the pressure and demands of the crowds into deserted places where he could spend long hours in prayer (4:42; 5:16; 9:18). Before he chose the twelve disciples who would form his inner circle, he "spent the night in prayer to God" (6:12). The Transfiguration occurred when Jesus had gone up on the mountain with Peter, John, and James "to pray" (9:28).

On the night before his death, he wrestled with the will of God on the Mount of Olives, praying earnestly and in anguish, his sweat becoming like great drops of blood falling on the ground (22:39-45). On the cross, he prayed for those who killed him and for you and me: "Father, forgive them; they do not know what they are doing" (23:34). Jesus saturated his life in the gracious reality of God.

The disciples witnessed the effect of Jesus' prayerful immersion in the Divine. They saw the connection between him and the one he called his "Father," and they knew that this tender bond was the source of Jesus' wisdom and power. His character was transparent to the presence of God; his heart was open to the love of God; his mind was infused with the truth of God; his spirit participated in the Spirit of God. Jesus' whole life was centered and focused on God, and his disciples knew that prayer was the discipline by which he rooted and grounded himself in the Divine. It's no wonder, then, that they said to him, "Lord, teach us to pray." That may well be the request we most need to make of Jesus: "Lord, teach us to pray."

Most simply and most profoundly, Jesus shows us that prayer is communication between us and God. It is a mind-to-mind, will-to-will, and heart-to-heart dialogue that deepens our relationship with God. Prayer is conversation held in communion. Most often, it is communication about our needs. Prayer is a way for us to bring to God the tangle of our life's choices, fears, and desires and, with God's help, sort them out.

We come, as the Lord's Prayer guides us to come, with an aching need for love and security, and Jesus teaches us to pray, "Our Father." We want to know that there is someone some-where who loves us completely and unconditionally, whose love will strengthen us and not drain us, will help us and not hurt us, will shelter us and not expose us. As we bring this need to God, talking about how it drives and drains us, God reassures us, and over time it becomes more and more believable that God cares for us like a strong mother and a tender father. We learn that when we are afraid and alone, crying out in the night, God rushes, just as our mothers rushed, to our sides, brushing the hair from our eyes, holding us close, and saying, "I'm here. Everything will be all right." When we venture out into the world, taking on some new and important challenge, we see God in the stands cheering us on, just as our fathers did, telling us, "You can do it. I believe in you."

We come to God with our need to see justice done and peace established, and Jesus teaches us to pray, "Your kingdom come." We lament that we live in a world where children go hungry—for food or for hope or for both. We insist that it is not right that the nations of the earth spend more on bombs and bullets than on books and medicines. We tell God that it is wrong to let the powerful ones of the earth run roughshod over the weak and help- less. As we pray, God gives us a vision of how God wants this world to be, how it will be when God's reign is established, and inspires us to act as if that world were already here. We find words for our need to see justice done and peace established: "Your kingdom come."

We come to God with our concerns for the people around us whom life has broken and bruised, and Jesus teaches us to pray, "Your will be done." We speak to God of the pain we see in the lives of those whose bodies are torn and tormented by sickness and suffering, whose hearts are darkened by the shadows of grief and loss, and whose minds are confused by the bewildering noise and blistering pace of life. Again, God shows us the divine intention: lives made whole, hearts reassured, and minds illumined by truth.

We come to God with our own smaller, but no less real needs: our need for regular reassurance that God is involved in the daily round of our lives. "Give us our daily bread," Jesus invites us to pray, a request that is shorthand for all God's daily blessings. Over the long stretch of our lives, we are given work to do and strength and wisdom with which to do it, food to eat and people with whom to share it, and glimpses of beauty to enrich the ordinary moments of our lives. Daily bread, daily provision, comes to us from the hands of a generous God.

We come to God with our sins—the burden of our guilt and the shame of our failure—and we pray, "Forgive us our sins, as we forgive those who have sinned against us." We acknowledge the ways we have fallen short of the glory God intends for us, the ways our sins have distracted us from God's will and diverted our gifts and energies from God's purposes for us. "Forgive us our sins." We hear God telling us we are forgiven, to go and sin no more, and we feel God setting us on our feet again and guiding us in a new direction.

As we spread before God the vast and various needs of our lives, we pray with joy and celebration, with grief and regret, with yearning and longing, with desperation and confusion. We offer God our lives because we trust that God loves us and can make something of this tangled bundles of choices, desires, and needs that we are.

Deacons, like other followers of Jesus, need to claim the gift of personal and private prayer. Without it, their own awareness of God's presence and love in all the dimensions and demands of their lives will diminish. They will lack the spiritual and emotional energy to live and lead in the ways God hopes and intends for them. Deacons also have the opportunity and responsibility to make the needs of the church, its leaders, and its members and participants a part of their prayers. To do so is a silent, unseen, but powerful way to serve.

# Individual Exercises

1. Does your practice of public and shared worship challenge our culture's assumptions, patterns, and expectations? If so, how?

2. What would it be like to offer your "entire self" to God? Try listing the components of your entire self. Does the list continue to grow? Does it include the elements of your public and private self? What do you think God might do with each item on your list?

3. In Jesus' life, there are "rhythms of prayer." What are your "rhythms of prayer"?

4. In the model prayer, Jesus instructs us on how to have conversation with God. Which parts of this prayer do you pray most frequently? Which parts do you pray less frequently?

5. In the model prayer, Jesus teaches us that God loves us completely and unconditionally. How do you open yourself to receive God's love?

6. Prayer is communication between us and God. In communication, we both speak to God and listen to God. How do you listen to God?

# Group Conversation

1. Discuss meaningful experiences of worship from your past and present. What elements of corporate worship are most important to you? To your family? To your church?

2. Do you prepare for corporate worship? If so, how?

3. Reflect on your practices of private prayer and discuss how each of you might grow in the practice of prayer.

4. Who has influenced you the most in corporate worship? Who have been your models or mentors in the practice of private prayer?

# Deacons Practice Partnership in God's Mission

All around us, people scramble for meaning and search for purpose. They wonder who they are and why they are here. You can see the questions in their eyes and feel them in your own heart: Is life about more than getting up every day, working and playing until time for bed, and then doing it all over again the next day until we die? Is there a reason for life? Is it headed anywhere or nowhere? Who am I? Why am I here?

In response to these kinds of questions, the church is called to make disciples. Matthew's Gospel ends with the risen Christ giving this familiar "great commission" to his followers: "Go therefore and make disciples of all nations, baptizing them in the name of the Father, and of the Son, and of the Holy Spirit, and teaching them to obey everything that I have commanded you." One of the privileges and responsibilities of being a deacon is to help the church keep this commission central to its life and ministry and to encourage the congregation to see itself as a community of God's partners in the mission of reconciliation.

What images do you have of a disciple? I see a huge flannel board resting on a not-very-stable easel. The easel was at the front of a dimly lit classroom. Around it were a dozen or so small wooden chairs occupied by an assortment of boys and girls who were more or less listening to the kindly woman who told us about Jesus' first followers—his disciples. She said that there were twelve, and she put their pictures on the board as she calls their names: Simon, called Peter; Andrew, brother of Peter; James, son of Zebedee; John, brother of James; Philip; Bartholomew; Thomas; Matthew the tax collector; James, son of Alphaeus; Thaddeus; Simon the Zealot; and Judas Iscariot, the betrayer. All of them were dressed in what looked like old men's bathrobes and sandals; each of them had a beard; and, other than that, they looked astonishingly like the men who were deacons in the First Baptist Church of Conley, Georgia, the church of my childhood. These flannel-board Sunday school characters are my earliest images of disciples of Jesus Christ.

I didn't know enough in those days to ask why there were no women on the flannel board or why the disciples' skin was the same color as ours. Later, of course, I learned that more pictures could have gone up on that board. Jesus had more disciples than the Twelve; many of his closest followers were women, and Middle Eastern people don't look like Georgians. I also learned that Jesus wanted my picture on that board. He wanted me, and everyone else, to be his disciple.

A disciple is someone who claims Jesus Christ to be lord and leader of their lives, someone who learns from Jesus who they are and why they are here, and someone who stays close enough to Jesus to follow him—to hear his voice and to observe his actions. Disciples allow Jesus to change their lives—to transform them into people who think as he thinks, respond as he responds, and feel as he feels. Disciples learn the meaning and purpose of their lives from Jesus. Jesus tells us who we are: we are beloved children of God in whom God takes great delight; and he tells us why we are here: to become people who know and share the love of God, give and receive grace and mercy, and experience and share hope and joy.

When someone decides to become a disciple of Jesus—to live as a follower of Jesus—the church symbolizes and seals that decision with baptism. Jesus said, "Go and make disciples by baptizing them in the name of the Father, and of the Son, and of the Holy Spirit." In one way, of course, baptism is about water: we immerse people in water and lift them up again; it's a way of showing what will happen to them in their lives with Jesus: their old, sinful, and confused lives will die and be buried, and their new, forgiven, and renewed lives will be raised up. The water matters because it dramatically enacts the miracle of resurrection that Jesus performs in his followers, but it is not water that matters most. What matters most is the experience that leads to the water: taking the plunge into the river of divine grace, being immersed in and surrounded by God's love and mercy, and experiencing the cleansing, refreshing power of God's forgiving and renewing presence.

So the church makes disciples by inviting people to the experience symbolized by baptism, and the church makes disciples by teaching them to obey everything Jesus has commanded us. We do not become instantly and automatically Christ-like at the moment we decide to follow him. Becoming like Jesus involves continual learning and growing, obeying and repenting, succeeding and failing. In many ways, it seems that every day is the first day of our discipleship because, as we learn about who Christ is and who we are, we also learn how little we know.

Thomas Merton noted that "in the spiritual life, there are no tricks and no short cuts . . . . Those who think they 'know' from the beginning will never, in fact, come to know anything. . . . We do not want to be beginners. But let us be convinced that we will never be anything else but beginners all our life!"[8] So the church teaches; it encourages us to keep hearing and responding to the living voice of Jesus Christ, who meets us in the Scriptures, in the vital traditions of our Christian past, and in the challenges of contemporary life.

## Conversation and Compassion

In response to questions people have about who they are and why they are here, we invite people to become disciples. Inviting, of course, involves talking—not just talking to them but talking with them in depth; and not just talking about their lives but talking about our own lives with Jesus and about what we most urgently believe and most fondly hope. The great commission depends on voices, and, as Tom Long claims, we are suffering from "laryngitis in the house of faith."[9] Finding our voices again is crucial, and the recovery of our voices depends on several things:

Remembering with gratitude the sound of the voices that called us to Christ. Where would we be if they had not found the courage and the love to speak to us?

Experiencing a renewed awareness of the difference grace is making in our lives. Who would we be if we had not learned that God loves us, forgives our sins, and gives us a reason to live that includes a reason to die?

Imagining what the lives of our friends and neighbors and colleagues could become if they experienced grace. How would their lives be changed and enriched if we could find a way to speak to them of Christ?

In far too many places, the church speaks with a voice that Jesus would not recognize as his: harsh, legalistic, and condemning. It is tragic when Christians who know the joy of grace and the freedom of faith have voices that are timid and weak, raspy and uncertain. Our world is hungry for the true gospel. It needs and wants the meaning and purpose Jesus offers. In response to that hunger, that need, we invite people to follow Jesus.

People aren't just asking "why" and "what"; they are asking "how": how can I go on with this hurting in my heart and this burden on my back? The world often seems to be trapped in a downward spiral of misery. Wars and rumors of wars. Despair and violence in the inner cities. Poverty in Appalachia. Persistent racism. Couples who push against each other by day and seethe against each other by night. Single parents who struggle to do what is right while feeling overwhelmed by the odds against them and their children. Illiteracy. Unemployment. Underemployment. Workaholism. Sickness. How do people cope? How do they find the strength and courage to live life without despair? How can they find healing for their hurts?

In response to the wounds people carry, the church is called to be God's partners in sharing the healing compassion of Jesus. To be compassionate means to feel our way into what it is like to live in another's skin, to face his or her limitations and challenges, to feel his or her hopes and fears. Jesus was a man of great compassion. In a compressed description of his characteristic way of conducting ministry, Matthew tells us, "Jesus went through all the towns and villages, teaching in their synagogues, preaching the good news of the kingdom, and healing every kind of disease and sickness. When he saw the crowds, he had compassion on them, because they were harassed and helpless, like sheep without a shepherd" (Matt 9:35-36). Compassion was Jesus' response to brokenness and helplessness, and it is to be the response of the church.

Since we are the church, we cannot blind ourselves to the struggles of those who are barely holding life together in the face of gnawing self-doubt, aching anxiety, and despairing paralysis. We cannot deafen ourselves to the cries of people who are on the margins: we feed the hungry, clothe the naked, visit the sick, lonely, and imprisoned, and shelter the homeless. We respond to the pain of our society with hope and help.

Deacons allow their hearts to be broken by the conditions that also break the heart of God. As servant leaders in the congregation, they also encourage the church to be God's faithful partners in reconciling the estranged and healing the wounded. They help the church to use its creativity, imagination, and resourcefulness to make a healing, hope-giving difference in the world.

We also make disciples by "putting on Jesus." I'm sure you've noticed the question that breathless reporters ask stunning stars on the red carpet: "And who are you wearing?" It's an odd question— not *what* are you wearing but *who*. The answers are something like, "I'm wearing Gucci" or "Versace" or "Vera Wang."

The Apostle Paul often wrote about "wearing" Jesus—about "putting on" Jesus. In Galatians 3:27, he said, "As many of you as were baptized into Christ have clothed yourselves with Christ." In Ephesians 4:24, he said, "Clothe yourselves with the new self, created according to the likeness of God." And in Colossians 3, he said,

> You have stripped off the old self with its practices and have clothed yourselves with the new self, which is being renewed in knowledge according to the image of its creator. . . . As God's chosen ones, holy and beloved, clothe yourselves with compassion, kindness, humility, meekness, and patience. Bear with one another and, if anyone has a complaint against another, forgive each other; just as the Lord has forgiven you, so you also must forgive. Above all, clothe yourselves with love, which binds everything together in perfect harmony. (3:12-14)

We become like Jesus by putting on Jesus; and, just as we get dressed every day, we put on Jesus day by day as we practice relating to the world and to other people as he would. We respond to the possibilities and problems of our lives in the ways we imagine he would. New Testament scholar Leander Keck suggested that we approach every circumstance with our own version of this question:

"What is the appropriate thing to do and be in light of the kind of person Jesus was?"[10]

Jesus had a radical commitment to the equality and dignity of all human beings. He was restless for people on the bottom and on the fringes of society to know that they could claim the joy, self-respect, and potential of children of God. He treated women with unprecedented respect and invited them to be his followers. He blessed and celebrated children, and he called attention to their openness and vulnerability as examples for all who would follow him.

Jesus was overwhelmingly generous with mercy for the broken, grace for the guilty, and welcome for the ashamed. He was tender with people's weaknesses and compassionate with their failures. His only harshness was toward those who were harsh with others. To everyone else, he said a version of what he said to the woman caught in the act of adultery: "I do not condemn you. Go your way, and from now on, do not sin again" (John 8:11).

Jesus had a vision of God's kingdom as a place and time where what God wants for the world and for human beings happens. He dreamed of earth restored, justice done, violence vanquished, peace experienced, illness healed, poverty ended, the marginalized welcomed, the guilty forgiven.

In light of who Jesus was, his vision of God's kingdom, what he did, and what he taught, how should we live? We "put on" Jesus by asking, in all the challenges and opportunities of life, "What is the right thing to do because of him?"

# Individual Exercises

1. Inviting people to become disciples of Jesus is a privilege. Who invited you to become a disciple of Jesus? Who influenced you in becoming a disciple or encouraged you after you became a disciple? How did they do it?

2. Can you give an example from the past where you "found your voice" when you talked with someone about your life with Jesus and what you most urgently believe?

3. In the context of your community, where is your church acting like Jesus in ways you can celebrate?

4. In the context of your community, explore the ways your church should act more like Jesus?

5. Outside your congregational and community context, where is your church acting like Jesus in ways that you can celebrate?

6. Outside your congregational and community context, where should your church explore the vision of Jesus for the kingdom of God?

# Group Conversation

1. What does your church do to engage friends from various backgrounds and help them find their place in your congregation? What could you do differently to welcome and receive people from various backgrounds into the life of your congregation?

2. Is your church a friendly church? Does your church know how to nurture true friendships?

3. Discuss ways your church currently gets to know its neighbors, and brainstorm some new ways your church can get to know them.

4. Honestly evaluate your congregation's efforts at evangelism and ministry in the community.

# Deacons Practice Creative and Generous Stewardship

The gift of life and the gifts that sustain life call for a grateful response from us. We call that grateful response "stewardship." Stewards recognize that who they are and what they have—including resources of money, time, gifts, talents, and influence—are entrusted to them by God. In a sense, those resources of energy, ability, and finances always belong to God, but God also leaves us free and responsible to make decisions about the use we will make of them. We have the opportunity to invest ourselves gladly, gratefully, and creatively in a partnership with God and God's people, a partnership of mission and ministry that extends the good news of God's loving reign and gracious rule.

Jesus didn't call his followers to take up "new" disciplines. For faithful Jews of Jesus' time (and it's crucial to remember that Jesus was a faithful Jew), genuine piety had three essential elements: giving offerings for those in need ("alms," Matt 6:2-4), engaging in prayer, (6:5-15), and fasting (6:16-18). Jesus assumed that his disciples would engage in all three: "Whenever you give alms . . . Whenever you pray . . . Whenever you fast . . ." (6:2, 5, 16).

Jesus did, though, urge his followers to pay close attention to their motives for engaging in these practices with which they were already familiar: "Beware of practicing your piety before others in order to be seen by them; for then you have no reward from your Father in heaven" (6:1). Jesus cautioned his followers about the craving for recognition of their faithfulness, and he encouraged them to insulate themselves from praise for their good works. They were called away from the applause of others and drawn toward the affirmation of God.

Those whose motivation was "to be seen and praised by others" went to great lengths to draw attention to themselves: sounding the trumpet before giving alms (6:2); arranging to be on the street corner or in the synagogue at prescribed times of prayer (6:5);[11] praying lengthy prayers loaded with impressive but empty words (6:7); and looking "dismal" to draw attention to their fasting (6:16).

By contrast, the disciples, whose reason for engaging in acts of piety was to respond faithfully to God's love, were to give their alms unostentatiously—not to "let their left hand know what their right hand is doing" (6:3). Jesus taught his followers to offer their personal prayers in seclusion and solitude, away from the eyes and ears of others (6:6), and to voice their public prayers in straightforward and unadorned words, confident that God was attentive to their needs (6:7-8). They were to fast without announcing that they were and to take care to appear radiant and joyful (6:17). These practices of piety, done with an eye only for God's approval, would be seen and rewarded by the "Father who sees in secret" (6:4, 6, 18).

As we explore the practice of generous stewardship of our entire lives, we will keep in mind and heart that our motives are not to be seen and applauded by others. Rather we will allow our minds and hearts to respond to God's love for us, to grow in our faithfulness, and to become more effective as leaders.

# Money and Material Possessions

Stewardship involves money, of course; and, in the Sermon on the Mount, Jesus sharply contrasted two ways of living. He said we can either invest our lives in "treasures on the earth" or in "treasures in heaven" (see Matt 6:19-21). We can serve either God or money, but not both (6:24). We live in a culture firmly committed to accumulating "treasures on earth," to serving money, and to the ways of competition and consumption.

Jesus wants us to have a realistic view of money, and he talked about its possibilities and limits, what it can and can't do for us, and how it affects us: "Do not store up for yourselves treasures on earth, where moth and rust consume and where thieves break in and steal; but store up for yourselves treasures in heaven, where neither moth nor rust consumes and where thieves do not break in and steal" (Matt 6:19-20). In other words, money and the things it can buy are impermanent. It might take a Mercedes a long time to rust away, but it will rust, just as surely as will a Ford Fiesta. Moths will eat a Brooks Brothers suit with as much gusto as they will chew on a pair of Carhart jeans. A thief can steal the diamond ring you inherited from your grandmother or the power tools you worked overtime for weeks to afford.

Things don't last, Jesus said. Because they don't, it's not wise to expect that they do anything of lasting significance for us. Money can feed hungry people, but it can't help us when we are starving for love. Money can build houses, but it can't take our hearts home. It can make us more comfortable, but it can't make us more content. Money can provide good medical care, but it can't do anything about our fear of death. That's why Jesus invites us to invest our lives in things that last forever—in treasures in heaven, treasures in faith, hope, and love.

Because there are limits on what money and things can do for us, Jesus cautions us not to turn money into a goal or a god. Money is a means, not an end. A tool, not a purpose. A resource, not a reason to live. Use money; serve God and other people. Don't use God and other people to serve or to make money.

Money is a symbol we use to make the exchange of goods and services easier. It's a symbol of how much time and energy we give to earn it. A hundred dollars is worth however much sweat and effort it takes to get it. So we don't really pay for things with money; we pay for them with our lives. We don't really give money, either; we give ourselves concentrated into the coins, bills, and checks we use to pay for things and experiences.

We spend our money—our life energy—to buy things. We *need* some of the things we buy, things like food, clothes, shelter, and transportation. We buy other things because we *want* them: gigantic TVs, paintings, golf clubs, jewelry, Chia Pets, Legos, and collectible Pez dispensers. Over time, some things we want become things we're convinced we need, and maybe we do. Two generations ago, a family of four or more shared one bathroom in a house. Can you imagine that happening now? Is access to the Internet a nicety or a necessity these days?

Some of the things we buy, whether we needed them, wanted them, or both, make statements about us. They identify us, expressing who we are. For example, a car might not be just a car. After all, a Prius is a car and an Escalade is a car, but the people who drive a Prius and the people who drive an Escalade are each saying something about what's important to them. Their cars don't just *do* something—they don't just haul people from place to place—they *say* something.

We also spend our money—our life energy—to buy experiences: to hear Bruce Springsteen or the New York Philharmonic live; to see the Grand Canyon or to sit in a sidewalk café in Paris; to take in a Broadway play or to support the middle school's end-of-year production of *Annie*; to zipline down a steep gorge or to hike the Appalachian Trail; to take cooking lessons or to learn ballroom dancing.

As with things, so with experiences: they say something about us. You might enjoy a trip to your family's farm in rural Georgia as much as your friend enjoys an "ecotour" of Alaska. After the trips are over, you have a couple of bushels of corn to share, while your friend has breathtaking pictures and a letter of commendation from Greenpeace. Even though both you and your friend enjoyed your trips equally, and even if you didn't mean to make a statement, you did. The trips said something about you to other people.

As followers of Jesus, we want our use of money to say that we are passionate for God's kingdom—for the will of God to be done on earth as it is in heaven, for the ways of God to become, more and more, the ways of people. We want our money to say that mercy and justice, compassion and healing, grace and forgiveness, joy and freedom matter so much to us that we give ourselves generously for them. These are "God things," and we can trust God to provide what we need when we live for God things. Jesus said, "Strive first for the kingdom of God and his righteousness, and all these things—the things you most need—will be given to you as well" (Matt 6:33).

# Stewardship of Life

Our use of the gifts of time, energy, influence, and talent also "speaks" about our commitment to the mission and ministry of God in the world. We notice the tears beginning to pool in a friend's eyes, see the sag in his shoulders, hear the slight catch in his voice, and take time to listen to him.

We remember that next week it will have been a year since her mother died, and we send her a card to assure her that we haven't forgotten about the lingering grief she carries. We learn that the floor of a family's porch has weakened to the point of danger and that snow accumulates on their *inside* window sills, so we organize a team of people from the church to do badly needed repair work.

We hear that an elderly church member's husband is in the hospital, so we cut her grass, take a casserole to the house, or sit with him so that she can rest. We see guests who are sitting alone in the dining room at Family Night Supper on Wednesday night, and we take our tray to their table and get acquainted with them.

We give up an afternoon a week to tutor a kid who, without someone's help, will never get out of high school or out of the projects. We forgo a golf game to serve soup to the homeless.

These are acts of generosity, of stewardship, that express our commitment to God and God's kingdom and embody our love for God and neighbor.

Jesus knew that anxiety keeps us from putting God's kingdom first. He understood that, when the will and way of God become lower priorities for us, it's not because we meant for them to slip from first importance. It happens because we get worried that if we don't do things the way our culture says to do them—get all you can while you can and keep all you can for yourself—then there won't be enough for us.

So Jesus offers us the freedom to trust that God always gives us everything we need to live the lives God calls us to live. Jesus turns our eyes to the wonders of creation: to the birds of the air, whom God feeds, and to the lilies of the field, which God clothes with beauty. He asks, "Are you not of more value than the birds?" And, "If God so clothes the grass of the field, which is alive today and tomorrow is thrown into the oven, will he not much more clothe you?" (see Matt 6:25-30). Get outside and see the vast world God has made and loves. Nature doesn't worry: flowers don't fret; birds aren't weighed down by fear. They do what they are made to do. They bloom, they fly, and they live the life God gave them to live.

Our lives are gifts God gave us, gifts God wants us to enjoy, and gifts God will certainly sustain. "Do not worry," Jesus reassures us, "do not worry, saying, 'What will we eat?' or 'What will we drink?' or 'What will we wear?' Your heavenly Father knows what you need" (Matt 6:31-32).

Jesus knew, and wants us to know, that God is glad, good, and generous. With that kind of God, we can freely live our truest lives and joyfully give our most generous gifts. Deacons, like all other Christians, are discovering that freedom and joy; and, as they do, they provide encouragement for others in their congregations to practice stewardship of every dimension of their lives.

# Individual Exercises

1. Reflect on the anxiety you feel about money and how you have learned to trust God. Record some steps you might take to become less anxious and more generous.

2. How has being a deacon affected or changed your practices in financially supporting your church?

3. Where did you learn the practice of tithing or giving? Who taught you? Who set an example for you? Who mentored you?

4. Write down some goals for the stewardship of your life for the next five to ten years.

5. Recall specific instances in which you have used your money, time, or talents as an expression of your love for God. What offerings were most joyful for you to give? Which were most sacrificial for you to make? What impact did these have on your life, your faith, and your relationships? What did you learn from these experiences of stewardship?

# Group Conversation

1. Discuss 1 Timothy 6:6-10 and its teaching on contentment. How do we cultivate a quiet heart when it comes to money? How do we learn contentment? Consider "acting your way into a new way of feeling" about contentment.

2. Discuss 2 Corinthians 9:6-15 and its teaching about generosity. How can we cultivate a generous heart when it comes to money? Consider "acting your way into a new way of feeling" about generosity.

3. Discuss Matthew 6:19-34 and its teaching about both contentment and generosity.

# Notes

1. T. F. Torrance, "Service in Jesus Christ," in *Service in Christ: Essays Presented to Karl Barth On His 80th Birthday*, ed. James I. McCord and T. H. L. Parker (Grand Rapids MI: Eerdmans Publishing Co., 1966) 3–4.

2. Ibid., 14.

3. Edward L. Buelt, *A New Friendship: The Spirituality and Ministry of the Deacon* (Collegeville MN: Liturgical Press, 2011) 151.

4. C. E. B. Cranfield, "Diakonia in The New Testament," in *Service in Christ*, 42–43.

5. Elizabeth O'Conner, *Eighth Day Of Creation: Discovering Your Gifts and Using Them* (Waco TX: Word, 1971) 26.

6. William James, *On Vital Reserves: The Energies of Men and the Gospel of Relaxation* (New York: Henry Holt and Company, 1899, 1900, 1911) 45.

7. Cornelius Plantinga, Jr., and Sue Rozeboom, *Discerning the Spirits: A Guide to Thinking about Christian Worship Today* (Grand Rapids MI: Eerdmans, 2003) 131.

8. Thomas Merton, *Contemplative Prayer* (New York: Herder and Herder, 1969).

9. Thomas Long, "Preaching about Evangelism," in *Preaching in and Out of Season*, ed. Long and Neely Dixon McCarter (Louisville KY: Westminster/John Knox Press, 1990) 79.

10. Leander Keck, *Who Is Jesus?* (Columbia: University of South Carolina Press, 2000) 175.

11. Set times for prayer were 9:00 a.m., noon, and 3:00 p.m. See also Daniel 6:10.

# Appendix

## Guidelines for Facilitators of this Study

1. Choose a location for the group study. This will depend on the schedule you choose and also what people you plan to include (see guideline 6). Make it a comfortable space where people can feel relaxed. If desired, provide snacks and/or drinks.
2. Begin and end each meeting with prayer. Encourage daily prayer during the week for each participant.
3. If possible, invite co-facilitators to help with the group discussion. Perhaps the pastor or a staff minister could co-lead with a deacon.
4. Protect the confidentiality of everything shared, and maintain respect and mutual trust in every part of the conversation.
5. Before beginning group conversation exercises, ask if anyone wants to share reflections from the individual exercises.
6. Choose a schedule for group conversations. Here are some suggestions:

• Once a Week for 10 Weeks (Deacons Only)
Host a 60-minute introduction before the first week, and then hold one session per week, about 75 minutes each.

• One-day Retreat (Deacons Only)
Have the introduction prior to the day of the retreat. This is a
possible schedule:
8:30—gathering time (coffee and pastries)
9:00–12:00—sessions 1–3
12:00–2:00—lunch together and reflection
2:00–5:00—sessions 4–6
5:00–6:30—dinner together and reflection
6:30–9:30—sessions 7–9

• Overnight Retreat (Deacons and Their Families, if desired)
This option may require a location that can accommodate families
(possibly including children), and give them entertainment options
while deacons are in learning sessions. Have the introduction prior
to the day of the retreat. This is a possible schedule:
5:30–6:30—dinner together (could include families)
6:30–9:30—sessions 1–3
8:00–9:00—breakfast together
9:00–12:00—sessions 4–6
12:00–2:00—lunch together and reflection
2:00–5:00 sessions 7–9
5:00—family gathering/dinner/adjourn

• Three Saturday or Sunday Meetings
Choose one. If desired, the group could gather for a meal before or
after each group of sessions.
9:00–1:00—Saturday mornings (sessions 1–3, 4–6, and 7–9)
OR
1:00–5:00—Saturday or Sunday afternoons (sessions 1–3, 4–6,
and 7–9)